Life in Erie's Fourth Ward

DAVID PAUL HOLMSTROM

INTRODUCTION

About five years ago I was watching a program on the History Channel about a family that came to the United States in the early1900's. It told about their life, the good times, the problems and struggles that they experienced in their new world. It was a fascinating story.

While watching this program I got to thinking that it would be interesting to write not only about my life but life in general in the Fourth Ward of Erie, PA during the 1940's and 1950's but also to pass on some of the family stories that I had heard from my mother, grandmother, step-grandfather, aunts and uncles.

It wasn't for just reasons of my own, but as a matter of letting my children, their children and future generations know what it was like living in those times. Something you wouldn't necessarily find in your high school history books.

For clarification the City of Erie was divided into Wards. The Fourth Ward was from State Street West to Cranberry Street and North from Sixth to the Bay front. Each Ward had a representative on City Council. The representatives were known at that time as Alderman. So each ward had representation on City Council.

ACKNOWLEDGMENTS

I would like to thank my awesome wife, Becky, for her support and encouragement to pursue this project. I also wish to thank my daughter Kristin (Holmstrom) Lane, for the endless hours she spent editing, correcting and organizing the material. My daughter, Victoria (Holmstrom) Whalen for her creative sketches that enhance the story. My sister, Shirley (Holmstrom) Wagoner, and my brother, Ken Holmstrom, provided some welcomed information that greatly helped to make the story more complete. For this I was thankful. Last, but not least, I wish to thank my cousin, Ralph Schauble, and his wonderful wife, Janet, for their input and support.

CHAPTER 1

That Which Does Not Kill Us

I was born Monday June 3rd, 1940 11:30am at Hamot Hospital in Erie, Pennsylvania. I was a light weight (6lbs. 5oz.) My dad, mom, two sisters (Shirley and Janet) and I lived in a small apartment in the back of a barber shop at 854 West 3rd Street just west of Liberty Street in Erie, PA. At the time I was born, whooping cough was going around. Shirley and Janet got it and so did I. Being frail, small and only six weeks old, it hit me particularly hard. Dr. Beck didn't have much hope for me and told my mother that I probably wouldn't make it. I surprised them though. But even good news took a long time to get around the neighborhood back then.

Years after my bout of whooping cough, in April of 1966, my brother Ken and I stopped for a beer at the Cascade Social Club on 3rd and Cranberry Street. Ken got to talking to an elderly lady sitting next to him at the bar. We had come to find out the lady knew our parents well. They talked for a while. Then, out of nowhere, the woman said to Ken that she was wondering if his brother died from whooping cough. She said that the last she heard was that Dave was very sick and heard he wouldn't live. Ken very calmly said, "He made it. In fact, this my brother Dave." The woman turned white as a ghost.

My mother, Ruth (Schauble) Holmstrom, was a small lady of German background. She stood 4' 10" tall. She wore a size 4 shoe and would buy her shoes in the children's shoe department. Mom was born blind but eventually gained her vision. My grandmother told the story of how they had to care for her in her blind condition. One day while my mother, who was eighteen months old at the time, was sitting at the table in her highchair. She started grabbing for some bright red apples in a bowl sitting on the table. They knew at that point she was able to see. However, Mom always wore very thick full vision glasses.

My mother went to school up to the eighth grade. Back then, for most girls, that was enough. Because of the depression, young women were needed to go to work at whatever kind of job they could find and bring money into the house.

During the depression, my mother went to some formal training sponsored by the government. The training involved learning home-making skills, cooking, baking, sewing, first aid and raising children.

My dad was 100% Finnish. He was average build and stood about 5'8" tall. He graduated from Erie Technical High School (a trade school) with a degree in auto mechanics in 1926 at the age of 16. Dad was a good man and worked long, hard hours as an auto mechanic. He always had work. I learned later that he was one of the best auto/truck mechanics in town. When Dad was with us, he was always joking and showing us magic tricks. He was always gentle and never mean to my mom or us kids.

But along with his amiable personality and love for his family, he lacked a sense of responsibility. It seems that when Dad would finally get off work, he wouldn't come home to his family, he would head for the bars or social clubs and drink. On occasion he would "test drive" a customer's car and end up going on a three-day bender. My mother would get calls from his boss wanting to know, "Where in the world is Walter?". Eventually he would show up and return the car. He would either get chewed out or fired. But Dad always got another job.

In reflection, I think about Christmas of 1961, when I was home on leave from the Navy. I decided to go Christmas shopping at the Liberty Plaza. Just as I was finishing up and walking to my car, I spotted Uncle John, my dad's oldest brother, walking towards me. It was so good to see him. He was the kind of guy you just couldn't help but like. We talked a bit, then he suggested that we go have a Christmas drink. Sounded good to me so we went to a little bar on Peach Street. We talked a lot about my dad since it was that time of the year when our family really missed him.

John said that he could never understand their father (Grandpa Holmstrom). He told how Grandpa would come home from work and just zone in on my dad. He would verbally abuse him and beat him senseless. And on several occasions, my dad was kicked down the cellar steps and left to lie down there. Grandpa was just mean to him for no apparent reason. I've read that when a child is treated like that, they treat their children the same way. I can say that he was never like that to any of us kids or our mother. He was laid back and easy going.

But back to our young family - it finally came to a point where we had no money to buy groceries or pay bills. Mom couldn't work while caring for three kids. The country was just coming out of the "Great Depression" and there just weren't that many jobs or opportunities out there.

As a result, we were evicted from the apartment on West Third Street and since we had nowhere else to go, we were forced to move into my Grandma Schauble's home at 343 West 4th Street. She would only allow my mom and us kids to stay, (for a fee). Grandma was so mad at my dad because of his lack of responsibility, she wouldn't allow him to stay with us. So, Dad moved back home with his mother, Grandma (Holmstrom) Komula. She lived at 945 West 3rd Street in Erie. My dad was only allowed to see us when he brought money to my mom. My grandmother and step-grandfather would go out on Saturday night and my dad would sneak in to see us. Then he would leave before they came home. I remember one Saturday night they came home earlier than expected and caught my mom and dad sleeping together. My grandma was so upset she went into our bedroom and pulled him out of bed and chased him out of the house - not a pleasant scene.

I recall when my dad was visiting, there were times that he would pull the old glider rocking chair right up next to the floor model Majestic radio so that his right ear would be next to the speakers. He would be listening to his favorite mystery story while reading a Zane Gray Western. Dad was an avid reader. He had read the entire Bible when he was a young man. My sister Jan was like him in that respect. She could get totally immersed in a book for hours.

I remember standing behind him while he was reading. Behind his left ear was an opening. When he was around 8 years old he had a mastoid. It was the growth of a bone that if left would have penetrated the brain, affecting the brain function. The bone was surgically removed leaving that opening. I asked my Dad what that was and how did he get it. He told me that's where they installed his brains. I really believed him.

I was always in trouble! I was always sensitive, whining, crying and acting out. I made my mother and father a nervous wreck. They never knew what to expect next.

I did have a lot of trouble sleeping. I would toss and turn and roll my head back and forth to try to get myself to sleep. But what worked best was the sound of the 11pm whistles from the trains passing through Erie up on the 14th and 19th street tracks. To me it sounded so cold and mournful and yet soothing. I thought about those trains out there in the freezing cold rain, snow and wind, but I was warm and comfortable in my bed. It always worked. Sometimes, when it was too soon for the trains, the fog horns from the lighthouse out on Presque Isle Bay Entrance would sound and sooth me to sleep. The familiar and mournful sound was re-assuring to me.

I can vividly remember the night or early morning that Kenny was born. I was just a little over three years old and still in a crib. But I was big enough that I could climb out of the crib by myself. I woke up and had to pee really bad. But my dad and mother were in the bathroom. Her water had just broken, so she was not about to get out of there any time soon. Of course, I was whining and crying because I had to go so bad. My dad told me to go back to bed. I climbed back in the crib and laid down. It got to the point I just couldn't hold it any longer and I let loose. Between my mother and me that night, my dad had his hands full.

Speaking of that crib, I recall a near-miss when I was about four years old. It was Sunday morning and I awoke to hear my Uncle Ed and Aunt Julia out in the kitchen talking to my dad. Uncle Ed and Aunt Julia were my godparents. So usually when I saw them it was either my birthday or Christmas and they would bring a present. I was all excited and went leaping out of my crib. When I hit the floor, the plaster from the ceiling over my crib came down in one big chunk and landed in my crib. It just missed me by inches. It sure scared the daylights out of me. My grandmother was really upset about the ceiling! And no, they didn't bring me a present. They just came to visit my dad and mom.

Dad would do his best to take me off my mother's hands and give her a break. She had her hands full with a new baby (Kenneth) who came along July 12th,1943. I think I was about four years old my dad came over to take me for a bus ride. At that time a bus ride was considered a good family activity. We walked to the corner bus stop and waited. The bus was running late so we went into Steinbaugh's Delicatessen Store on the southwest corner of 4th and Chestnut Streets. There was a soda fountain counter in the back of the store. There you could get sodas, milk shakes, ice cream cones and frosted malts, (any soft ice cream). My dad knew the owner Charlie. We went back to the counter so my Dad could talk to him. I spotted a chrome cup sitting on the counter. Being small, I couldn't see what was in the cup. I struggled to reach up, pulled the cup off the counter and dumped a chocolate shake right down the front of me. Man, was my dad ticked. He cleaned me up and had to pay Charlie for the milk shake. He didn't want to take me home to change so we got on the bus just the way I was, a real mess.

Our stay at my grandma's was supposed to be temporary. At least until my dad got his act together. But it never happened. We would end up living at my Grandmother Schauble's house for the next 18 years.

CHAPTER 2

WWII – United for the Effort

I was born about a year and a half before World War II started. I don't remember news of the Japanese attack on Pearl Harbor or the fact that on the day after Pearl Harbor, Nazi Germany (Hitler) declared war on the United States.

However, I do have memories of the later years of the war 1943-1945.

Because of the war effort there were shortages of all the essentials like food, gasoline, coal, oil, metals, rubber, lumber, etc.

As a result, the government set up a rationing system. A family could buy coupons and tokens from a government agency. But you could only buy enough to provide for your family depending on the number and age of the family members. This was the government's way of controlling these essential commodities in support of the war effort.

On the other side, the local grocery stores were given an allotment of meat, sugar, and other basic food stuffs. The gas stations were given limited allotments of gasoline, tires and oil to supply the people in that particular ward.

Most homes at that time were heated with coal or heating oil. So those were controlled through rationing also. Some were heated with natural gas.

Everyone was very careful not to waste anything. Once your rations were gone there was no going back to get more until next month when the allocations would be replenished.

The government encouraged people to conserve. To supplement food supplies, they encouraged everyone to plant Victory Gardens, grow fruit trees, and raise chickens and rabbits. My grandparents had all of these.

We would walk to save gasoline. We would collect tin cans, rags, and newspapers. They even wanted the grease left over from cooking which could be used to make lubricants and oils for the military, nothing went to waste.

Like any other government program there was corruption. Cigarettes, gasoline, meat, heating oil and coal were particularly "Hot Black Market" items. If you knew the right people and had the money you could get the items outside the system. The store keepers would hold out too. They would save the best meats, vegetables, sugar and toiletries for friends and family.

Going to the grocery store with my mother to get our ration of meat, sugar and vegetables using our coupons and tokens was always a lesson in standing your ground. It seemed that every time we went, my mother would get into an argument with the store owner. He would claim that his monthly allotment was gone, and she'd have to come back next month. My mother would argue and raise Cain until she got what she wanted. She knew that he was holding out and she wasn't leaving until he gave in with the goods. As I think back the store owner would give in just to get us out of the store. I also think that was my mother's plan.

On the other hand, when she didn't win, we ended up going to another store in the neighborhood. At that time there was a grocery store on just about every corner. Sometimes we might go to three or four different stores to get everything. It wasn't a fun trip.

There was one super market. It was called the A&P (Atlantic and Pacific Tea Company) Super Market. But it was located on 8th and Walnut Streets. That was too far to walk and carry your groceries home.

There were times when things were sparse, and we were without food. It was the winter of 1943. It was a Sunday morning and my mother was still in bed. Shirley, Janet and I were in the kitchen looking for something to eat for breakfast. There was no cereal, eggs or milk. All we could find is a half loaf of white bread and some sugar in a bowl. So being the creative cooks that they were, Shirley and Janet made sugar sandwiches, a poor man's doughnut, yummy!

The City of Erie had a lot of critical war equipment production. GE was making locomotives and diesel engines. Lord Corporation was making various shock mount systems for reciprocating aircraft engines. Kaiser Aluminum was producing aluminum for aircraft structures. Every manufacturing facility in Erie had some part in the war effort.

In the 1960's and 70's I worked at Lord Corporation in the Inspection Department. My supervisor, Mr. Claire Cubitt, told me about what it was like working at Lord during World War II.

He said that the government had taken over the plant so that they could more closely control this critical commodity. The government chose the Navy to come in and run the facility for the duration. Everyone's work was closely watched. If there was any scrap found it was almost considered sabotage. There would be a full investigation to determine where, when and who caused the scrap. So, when a machine operator would accidentally make a bad part, rather than face the scrutiny of an investigation, he would simply throw the piece out through the open overhead window on to the roof.

After the war my supervisor was assigned the task of heading up a crew to go up on the roof and gather all the parts, box them up and bring them to the Inspection Department for sorting. The boxes of parts were stacked up to the ceiling against the back wall. It took them six months to sort through these parts. He said that better than 75% of the parts were salvageable.

As a precaution the government required that we have air raid drills, better known as "Blackouts". This was a drill where at night, when the sirens blew, everyone was required to draw their shades and turn out the lights. The purpose was to totally black out the city so that in the event of an air raid by Nazi Germany, Fascist Italy or the Japanese the city would not be visible at night from the air. It was enforced in every neighborhood by the air raid warden. If you did not participate you could be put in jail and fined. Already they had spotted Nazi submarines off the coast of Long Island, NY, Norfolk VA and Jacksonville, Florida. It was scary times.

When these blackouts would occur, my sisters Shirley, Janet and I would go out in the back kitchen and hide under the coats hanging on the rack. Of course, Shirley and Janet would start terrorizing me and telling me that the Nazis were coming to get me, and they loved to eat little boys. I was young and gullible and believed every word. It scared the daylights out of me.

I was 5 years old when World War II ended in 1945. The paper boys came down Fourth Street selling the Five Star Extra yelling that the war in Europe had ended. That day in May is now remembered as Victory in Europe (VE Day) and in August, Victory in the Pacific over Japan (VJ Day). I remember how excited my Aunt Helen was that Uncle Bob was coming home from Europe. He was shot up in France and was in the hospital in England recovering, when the Nazis bombed the hospital and he got wounded again. He managed to escape the hospital and helped several other fellow patients get out, saving their lives. He received a "Purple Heart". Finally, he was coming home, and he would be out of harm's way. He got home two days before his 22nd birthday on September 25th, 1945.

CHAPTER 3

The One-Armed Babysitter

My dad never got drafted. Under the guidelines, he was exempt because he was a married man with 3 children, an excellent auto/truck mechanic needed in his community and had a heart defect. Little did we know how serious this last exemption was.

During the war you couldn't buy a new car. Due to the war effort, all the auto manufacturers were converted over to manufacturing Jeeps, tanks, planes and ships. In fact, all manufacturing was converted to the war effort. If your car broke down (blown engine or transmission) you got it fixed. Hopefully they could find a used engine or transmission to replace it.

My dad worked long hard hours especially near the end of the month for State Inspection. The monthly inspection system was such that for example, if you have an inspection sticker on your windshield with a "2" on it the car was due for inspection the following year by the end of February. Times were tough, and money was hard to come by so people would wait until the last day to get their car inspected. That's when Dad would work 15 to 18 hours a day.

I can remember Mom telling how Dad was always there when one of us kids were born. Except when Janet was born. She was born on July 31st, 1938. Last day of July State Inspection. He couldn't get away.

One time he came over to visit my mom and told her that he had made over $3500 that year. He had worked a lot of hours. That was big money at the time. As I grew older and thought about this, I couldn't understand why my Dad wouldn't take care of us the way he should. He obviously had the money. But that was the way he was.

Dad would occasionally take me to work with him on Sunday. I remember one Sunday I was with him while he worked on an old car replacing the wheel bearings. The bearings on this car were like one inch in diameter steel ball bearings. One of the bearings came up missing. Everyone thought that I took it. I didn't. I was only four years old and had no idea what a bearing was. Anyway, I was searched. They looked in the car that my Dad was driving, but no luck. They never did find it. My dad went out back and got a ball bearing out of a junker and slapped the wheel back together. Problem solved.

On another Sunday, I was with Dad working late. We left the garage about 6:00 and on the way home we stopped at the Portuguese Club. Dad made me set at a side table across from the bar with a bottle of pop, while he sat at the bar with his buddies drinking beer. After a while, I started getting restless and going up to the bar and bugging Dad that I wanted to go home. Finally, he gave me a nickel and told me to go put it in the slot machine (One-Armed Bandit). (These were illegal in the state of Pennsylvania, but every club had them).

I was barely tall enough to put the money in the slot, let alone pull the handle down. Some old guy reached over and helped me pull it down. I could see the wheels spinning while standing right in front of the machine. The wheels stopped, and hundreds of nickels came pouring out of the machine hitting me in the face. I was terrified and started screaming and crying. My Dad saw what was happening and came flying across the bar room whipped out his knit cap, pushing me aside and catching the nickels. I had hit the jackpot; $25.00 in nickels. Big money at that time. He gave me six nickels and kept the rest.

Because I was young and curious I always managed to get into trouble. One Sunday morning (I was about four years old) I climbed up to my dad's top dresser drawer. I went through the drawer and found some interesting white balloons. I put them in my pocket. Later, Shirley, Janet and I had to go to Sunday School at 9:30 and then to church service at 11:00 at The Northwest Gospel Tabernacle. It was a neighborhood church, which was Baptist, located on the north side of the 500 block of West 4th Street. By the time we got to the 11:00 church service, I was pretty bored. I figured I could blow up my balloons and that would be fun. Suddenly, girls and women started screaming at me. Ushers were coming into the pew from both ends. They were trying to get my balloons. I cried and carried on, "I want my balloons back!" They picked me up and took me back to the reception room and tried to calm me down by bribing me with candy. They kept asking me where I got the balloons. So, I told them. They asked me if I had more and I showed them. They offered me more candy. Actually, the candy tasted much better than the balloons. The ushers gave Shirley the unopened packages of balloons and told her to tell my mother what happened when we got home. Shirley told Mom and David got his butt tanned good.

Since all our neighbors went to that same church, my mother was too embarrassed to even go out to hang laundry. Eventually that embarrassment faded, and things went back to normal.

Just outside the back-kitchen door was an attached storage shed. Then going through the shed out the back door and across the sidewalk was David's dirt pile. My mom would put me out there in the morning and I would play by myself for hours. I had my little cars and trucks and would build houses, bridges and roads out of sticks and twigs. It was my creative time.

I recall several times I was out there playing and having fun when all of a sudden, the sky would get dark, accompanied by a loud roaring of engines. There were hundreds of bombers or fighter planes flying over. There were so many planes that they cast a shadow partially blocking out the sun. This would last 15 to 20 minutes. I found out later that these planes were built in Chicago, Cleveland and Detroit and were being ferried to New York by women pilots. The fighter aircraft would be disassembled at the east coast and put on cargo ships headed for England. There the aircraft would be reassembled and readied for battle in Europe. Men would fly the heavy bombers to England. The first couple times I was terrified, but after a while I got used to it.

On Sunday afternoons, my dad might come over and visit. He would usually give my oldest sister Shirley the money to take us kids to the Gem Theater for the afternoon matinee. Usually it was a double feature with a 5-minute World News clip, a cartoon and a weekly adventure serial in the middle. These Serial Adventures were like 15-minute films with Roy Rogers and Dale Evans, Gene Autry, the Durango Kid, Hop-a-long

Cassidy and the Cisco Kid. Each week they would end up in death defying situation. To see how they escaped and if they survived, you would have to come back next week. The double features were usually a Tarzan, Bud Abbott and Lou Costello (comedy), The Three Stooges, The Bowery Boys or a cowboy movie and then a war movie. Then again there might be two romance movies. To me that was boring. All that kissing and hugging stuff. Yuk! So being the free thinker that I was, I would decide to go outside. Sister Shirley would warn me that if I left they wouldn't let me back in unless I paid $.15. I figured I'd get back in. I would go outside and get bored there and try to sneak back in. Got caught every time. There I was stuck outside in the cold. I had to wait for Shirley and Janet to come out since I was not allowed to walk home alone. I did that a couple of times, then got wise.

The Gem Theater Building located on the north side of West Fourth Street just east of Cherry Street was unique. As I recall, it was owned by the Siebold Family. They lived in the apartment on the second floor. They ran the theater on the first floor and the Gem Social Club with four bowling alleys in the basement. Sitting in the theater was always a thrill. It smelled of burnt popcorn and a bit musty. You would be setting there and every once in a while, you might feel either a big mouse or a small rat run over your foot. One Sunday afternoon, while the movie was playing, a kid started screaming because a mouse ran up his pant leg. Guess that's how it earned its nickname the "Rat House".

The winter of 1944/1945 was a bad one. It snowed heavily just after Thanksgiving. Shirley and Janet got suited up and went outside and played in the snow.

My Mother wouldn't let me go out because the snow was too deep, and my legs were too short. I cried and carried on and finally she gave in. I got suited up and went outside. I waddled around and got to the middle of the backyard where I got stuck. The snow was up to my waist and packed all around my legs. I couldn't move. So, there I was screaming at the top of my lungs. My mother was only 4′ 10″ tall, so when she tried to come out and get me she got stuck. It ended up my step-grandfather had to come out and help her back to the house. Then he came out and got me. (cussing all the way).

CHAPTER 4

The House That Was Home

My grandparent's house at 343 West 4th Street was built in 1823. Originally it was built as a two-story frame building to serve as "The Erie Girls Dance Academy". Downstairs was the dance studio. As you come in the front door from the front walk you would walk straight past the stairway to a little side dressing room. The student dancers would get dressed in their dancing costumes and then proceed to the two larger rooms where lessons and practice dances were performed. On the second floor there were two rooms used for academy administration.

The house was bought and sold many times. There was a huge addition put on the back of the house somewhere around 1920. This gave the luxury of indoor plumbing including a flush toilet.

My grandmother, Bertha Schauble, and Lane (Pink) Weindorf, moved in together in 1934 and rented the house for 20 years.

Pink bought it in 1954. I remember him paying cash. The money even smelled musty. We had no idea where he kept the money, but it sure wasn't in the bank.

In late 1940, Mom, Shirley, Janet and I moved in. We had a small bedroom that was approximately 10'X10' on the first floor. We crammed in two twin beds, one full size bed, a chest of drawers, and a dressing table. It was real cozy and got even cozier when Kenneth and Donna came along. We had a small dining area in the back of the kitchen. Gram and Pink had a bigger dining area in the room next to the back kitchen. Gram and Pink had separate bedrooms on the second floor. But for the most part Gram always slept on the couch in their dining area. The house was heated with a pot belly coal stove in the corner of Gram's dining area. There was a gas stove located in the corner of the formal dining room. There was no heat in our bedroom or in our dining area, just the residual heat from the pot belly coal stove.

The refrigerator was an ice box (no electricity required). It was a heavily insulated wooden chest about 5' high by 3' wide by 2' deep. Inside was a huge 25lbs. block of ice setting on the top shelf. You would stack everything around the block of ice or on the lower shelf. There was no such thing as a freezer section. So all refrigerated food had to be consumed within a week or it would go bad. The iceman came around every day. There was a sign that the ice company provided. It was red and white maybe 14" square. On one edge there was a number 25, then on another edge was the number 50, then 75 on the next edge and 100 on the fourth edge. So, if you wanted 75 pounds of ice you would put the sign in the front window with the 75 at the top. The iceman could see from the street that you needed 75lbs. of ice and would bring it in to your house and put it in the icebox.

In the bathroom there was a gas fired side-arm water heater. That only got turned on Saturday afternoon for Saturday night baths. Otherwise during the week, we would heat water in a tea kettle and sponge bathe in the bathroom hand basin. It was crude by today's standard, but we made do.

On Monday, the water heater was fired up for laundry day. My mother's washer was a Blackstone washer with a power wringer. The washing machine was kept in the corner of our kitchen eating area. Mom would push the washer into the bathroom to do the laundry.

She would run hot water from the bath tub into the washer with a hose - add soap and clothes. Once the wash cycle was done she would then run the soapy wet clothes through the wringer into the bathtub filled with cold rinse water to soak the soap out of the clothes. She would then start another load in the wash machine. While that was running she would rotate the wringer out over the bath tub and run the wet soaking clothes in the bathtub through the wringer, catch them on the other side and put them in the clothes basket. (You had to be very careful that you didn't catch your hand in the wringer. It would rip your skin off). She would then take the clothes out and hang them in the yard on clothes lines. Sometimes there were so many clothes to hang out that my grandmother would have to move her car out to the alley to make room in the yard. The washing was an all-day process. On rainy or snow days my mother would have to string up clothes lines in our dining area. It would take a couple days to dry them. Then we would move down to the other end of the kitchen and have stand-up meals.

Our sleeping arrangements were unique. We all slept in the same bedroom with bare floors and colder than Siberia in the winter. When we first moved in, Mom had the full-size bed. I slept in a crib. Shirley and Janet slept in a twin bed. Then when Kenny came along he slept in a small cradle. When my dad died my mother was pregnant with sister Donna. When Donna came along our grandmother (Holmstrom) Komula and my dad's brothers and sisters bought us bunk beds and surplus army blankets. Kenny and I slept in the top bunk and Shirley and Janet slept in the bottom. Donna of course slept in a crib. But when Donna got big enough, she slept with Janet. Shirley slept in the full-size bed with Mom. You had to go into the bathroom to change or get dressed. If you could get in there.

It wasn't much, but I have to give my mother a lot of credit. She kept after us kids to clean-up and put our stuff away, just so we could get into the bedroom. By the same token she managed to keep us together as a family. She put up with a lot from my grandmother and step-grandfather. For years I resented my grandmother and step-grandfather because they seemed so mean to my mom and us kids. They charged my mother $45.00 a month rent, plus half the coal, gas and electric. The phone was half also, but only my mother was allowed to use it. Then if there was any other way Gram could weasel money out of her, it was fair game.

However, as I grew older I began to realize too, that they didn't have to take us in. My mother would've had to put us in an orphanage or split us up and put us in foster homes. In a sense we were lucky. They took us in and my mother was willing to put up with the aggravation that came with staying at Gram and Pink's house. My dad wasn't much help since my mom had to track him down every week to get money for food and bills. Between my dad, grandmother, grandfather and us kids, it was a rough life for my mother. But she was a tough German lady and handled it well.

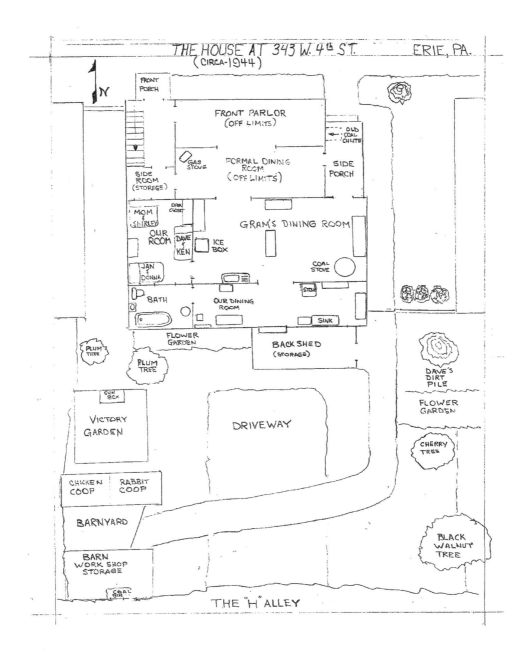

CHAPTER 5

Everything Changed but Nothing Changed

There was a time in the summer of 1946 when Dad told Mom that he had found a place to rent on Myrtle Street between 2nd and 3rd He was going to rent it and get us out of there. We were all excited. Shirley took us down there, so we could at least see what it looked like from the outside. But unfortunately, we never made the move. One excuse after another and after several weeks it all fell apart. Another disappointment for us and especially for my Mom.

It was the month and year, December 1947, that everything changed but nothing changed. On Sunday the 21st of December we were all at home rehearsing our Christmas poems for the Church Christmas Pageant that night at the Northwest Gospel Tabernacle. Dad showed up around 4:30 in the afternoon. We were all glad to see him. He helped all of us practice our poems. We laughed and played.

He used to pick me up by the waist and turn me upside down and have me walk on the ceiling. Dad would do this to me again on this night to start the fun. It terrorized the devil out of me. Kenny loved it. Of course, he was only four years old at the time. Then Dad made us a bet that for a penny he could stand on his head. We accepted the challenge.

So, he went to the corner by the cupboard and stood on his head. We said that was cheating. But he said no, he had stood on his head like he said he would. Then when he stood up we all started laughing because his hair was all messed up and in his face.

Later he took us into the front living room (the parlor) and played the piano and we sang Christmas songs. What a fun time!

We left for church about 6:30. Dad stayed with Mom. She was five months pregnant with Donna and not feeling good. The church pageant was over at 9:00 and we all hurried home hoping that Dad would still be there. Mom said that he had left and went to the Gem Club. (It was a social club in the basement of the Gem Movie Theater about two doors away from the Northwest Gospel Tabernacle. (I hope he looked in while we were performing). We were disappointed but hopeful that he would be back before we went to bed. However, he didn't come back by 10:00 so we went to bed since we had school the next day.

Shortly after midnight there was a knock on the front door. It was the Wagner couple. They told my mother that they had just left the Gem Club and found my father lying dead on the sidewalk. They had gone back into the Club and called an ambulance, but it was too late. My mother went into shock and nearly collapsed. Fortunately, my grandmother was there with her. By this time all of us kids were awake wondering what was going on. Shirley was allowed to get up but the rest of us had to stay in bed. About ten minutes later some detectives came to the house and talked to my mother. We were all in shock and disbelief. Shirley and Janet were hit particularly hard. Kenny and I were too young to understand the gravity of what had happened.

What did happen to our young father that night? Earlier in the evening he was standing on his head, playing piano, having fun with his kids in anticipation of Christmas then later in the evening found lying on the sidewalk. We discovered later when Dad had gone to the Gem Club that night. Dad and another guy were bowling. Since there were no pin boys, Dad would bowl, and the other guy would set pins. When the game was done they would switch. Earlier that week, Dad had dropped a car battery on his foot. His foot had swollen up quite a bit, but he chose to ignore it. Apparently, a blood clot had formed and through all this activity the clot broke loose and caused a heart attack.

The Funeral Home was at Hanley's on West 8th Street between Liberty and Poplar Streets. Visiting hours were 2 until 4 and 7 until 9. There were a lot of people there. Not only grandmothers, grandfathers, aunts, uncles and cousins visited, but many friends of the families.

I was seven years old and allowed to go to the funeral home once. I could just barely see my dad lying in the casket. I could see his hands crossed on his chest. I noticed that his left hand was up away from his right hand. The Funeral director would put his hand down and minutes later it would be back up. (Scary). In my young mind I thought it was like he was waving good-bye. Dad was buried on Christmas Eve the 24th. His birthday would have been on the 26th of December. He would have been 37.

It was a sad Christmas as would be expected. But the families and friends on both sides did everything possible to make it nice for my mother and us kids. We got a lot of food, clothes, toys and games. The Masons, Shriners, Salvation Army, the Lutheran Memorial Church, Marine Corp Toys for Tots. Everyone pitched in. Today all of us kids give back to these organizations and hope that we can make some children happy for the holidays. It is one of the main reasons I joined the Masonic Order, to give back.

Everything changed, but nothing changed. My mother didn't have a husband, we didn't have a father, and we didn't have an income. But when my Dad was alive we really didn't have those things.

My mother got hooked up with Social Security for us kids. Each one of us got an allotment each month. That also helped us to stay together. At that time there was also a Pennsylvania State Subsistence program called "Mother's Assistance". This program gave us an additional $30.00 a month. Later there was the Federal program called Surplus Food. The farmers would over produce, and the Federal Government would buy up this surplus food and distribute it to low income families. They had cheese, canned beef, pork and gravy, powdered milk, sugar, corn meal and butter. This helped a lot.

Then there was Farrell's Grocery Store on the southeast corner of 4th and Chestnut Streets. The store was operated by Guy and Liz Farrell. They were helpful in that they would extend credit to my mom each month. Especially at the end of the month when we had more month than money. We could go to Farrell's and get groceries and they would put it on my mom's account. There was a small ledger that we would take with us and they would keep track of the purchases each time we went. They had a matching ledger. Then at the beginning of the month when the Social Security check came in, my Mom would go to Farrell's and pay the bill off. One thing my mother told us kids, "You always pay your bills".

Life goes on. Donna was born April 19th, 1948. (Ironically Shirley was born on April 19th, 1937). I remember the day they brought Donna home from the hospital. What a doll. Everybody adored her, but who wouldn't. We all got a turn to hold her and later we all got a turn to watch her. She was a good baby. My step-grandfather treated her like a princess. She was the apple of his eye.

CHAPTER 6

The Paper Route

I turned eight years old in June of 1948. My Grandmother Schauble was constantly reminding me that I was the oldest boy and as such it was my duty to help my mother. So in August, I looked into getting a paper route. At that time, the newspaper bundles were dropped at the back end of the fire hall at 5th and Chestnut Streets. Then the paperboys would pick up their papers and deliver them on their respective routes. Each bundle had a route number marked on it.

I'll never forget when I went to my mother and asked her if I could get a paper route, my grandmother interrupted and said that was foolish. My mother didn't have that kind of money to pay for papers just so I could have fun delivering them. I was so dumbfounded by the statement, I just busted out laughing. Gram didn't appreciate that at all. Then I explained to them how it worked. You picked up your papers every day and delivered them. Then on Friday and Saturday you went to each of your customers and collected the money for the week's delivery. The daily paper was $.04 and the Sunday paper was $.15. So for the week it was $.39, or $.24 if you just took the daily paper.

But to the paperboy his cost for the paper was $.03 for daily and $.11 for the Sunday paper. And you were billed by the Dispatch Herald accordingly each week. When you paid your bill, whatever money that was left over was yours to keep. On average you should make $5 to $6 a week. For a little kid that was pretty good. During the week you delivered after school. Then on Saturday you could pick up your papers after 1:00PM. On Sunday you could pick up your papers after 3:00AM. That way you could deliver them early and make it on time for church.

On paper it looked like a good deal, if you had 75 to 80 customers. But many weeks it was a losing situation. Customers wouldn't pay and canceled the subscription.

Or they would move out and leave you holding the bag for 3 or 4 weeks' worth of unpaid newspaper bills. At that time, you as the paper boy absorbed the loss. Sometimes it would be as much as $4 or $5 in one week.

On the brighter side, there was Christmas and New Year's Holidays. The first year I got $125.00 in tips. The newspaper would sell calendars to the paper boys for $.03 each. Then we would take them to our customers and they would give you a little something for them. Most customers gave you anywhere from a quarter to a dollar. One customer asked me how much I paid for them and I told him. He gave me $.04. But every bit counted and helped to make up for the losses. My first route was #118 on Fourth Street from Chestnut to Sassafras. I had about 50 customers. It was considered a small route. But between Christmas and the newspaper's annual calendar I made out very nicely. It helped my mom a lot at Christmas time.

I took the route from John Webster, one of my class mates in second grade. I worked with John for a week before I took over. On the first day it was raining hard. The papers were in a canvas bag in the wagon. There was a clip book that had a card for each customer on the route. They were in the order in which the papers were to be delivered. After the first delivery I was looking at the clip book and dropped it. All the cards went flying out of the book and all over the sidewalk. I panicked. The cards were all messed up and out of order. I started to choke up but got a grip and started picking up the cards and putting them into the clip book. I figured I would fix them up later. Then I started to deliver from memory. It went well. That started my eight-year career as a paperboy and salesman.

The newspaper would hold contests. For each new subscription you got, you would get credits. For instance, ten credits for a new daily subscription and 25 credits for a new subscription for the daily and Sunday paper combination. I managed to get a lot of new subscriptions and won enough credits for a jack knife, camping equipment, a BB gun. If you got 26 new subscriptions, you could win a bike or an all-expense paid trip to Chicago or New York. I earned three Bikes and a trip to Chicago for a week. I also won some trips to Cleveland for baseball games and to Buffalo for the Ice Follies.

After a year or so, I took a route on West Third Street from Chestnut to Cherry Streets. It was a bigger route and better residential customers.

This was a route that had some good and not so good memories. One day I was delivering on Cherry Street just off Third Street. At this one customer's house the old woman was bed ridden in a high hospital bed. Her son asked me to take the paper into her every day. Which I did. This one summer afternoon I went in and found that she had fallen out of bed. She was lying on the floor and moaning and in a lot of pain. I was a 90 lb. 9-year old and could hardly move her let alone pick her up. I knew her son worked at General Electric, so I tried calling there to let him know what had happened. I didn't realize how big GE was. The operator kept asking me what department he worked in. Of course, I had no idea. Suddenly, her son came into the house yelling at me, wanting to know what I was doing. I tried to explain to him what happened. But he wasn't listening. He chased me out of the house. (I was glad to get out of there).

The next day I wasn't sure what I should do as far as taking the paper into the old woman. But when I got to the house the son was there and came to the door. He apologized for his reaction the day before. He didn't realize what I was trying to do and overreacted and was very sorry. I asked him if his mother was hurt. He said no, bruised a little, but O.K. He said that she had told him what happened and that I was trying to help. He asked me if I would continue to bring the paper into the house to his mother. I of course told him I would.

Then there was an old woman who lived in a small cottage behind Kavalage's Department Store on 4th and Cherry Streets. She wasn't one of my customers but every day when I was finished with my route I would walk by her house on my way home. She was always at her window and would wave to me. I would wave back. She was old and looked a little scary, but I waved anyway. One Sunday morning I finished delivering and walking past her house and the door opened. She had a box of chocolate eclairs and asked me if I would like one. I was a little skeptical, but I took one. She asked me if I would like a glass of milk with the eclair. I said no, thanked her and went on my way. The next Sunday the same thing. Only we talked a little more. Then it was every Sunday. She actually was a sweet old lady and lonely for someone to talk to. A couple months passed, and we became good friends. I would leave a Sunday paper for her. I always had one or two left over. Then one Sunday I came by her house and the curtains were drawn and lights were out. I figured she was still sleeping so I just left a paper inside her storm door. I kind of watched the house for the next week but the curtains remained drawn and lights out. I found out later that she had passed away.

Sunday delivery was not all that thrilling. You would get up about 4:30am go out in the cold rain or snow and deliver. The thing that ran through my mind was that those lucky people that I'm delivering to are nice and warm snuggled in their beds and I'm out here soaking wet, freezing my back side. Just so they can have their newspaper with their morning coffee. But then again, there was the Christmas and New Year's tips that made it all worthwhile.

The paper route experience was both good and bad. I had a lot of good customers and a small number not so good. I had bicycles stolen, newspapers and all. But the incident I recall most vividly was being robbed of $ .39.

I was delivering papers on a Saturday afternoon in the 100 block of West 8th St. A big kid approached me and was real friendly. He wanted to know if he could help me deliver. I was 11 years old at the time and knew enough that something was not right. I was very suspicious. I told him no, I was just about finished. So, he asked, "Do you mind if I walk with you". I told him that I didn't mind. So, I continued to deliver papers with him tagging along. When I got to Sassafras St. I started up towards ninth street. He followed.

About half way up the block he pulled a switch blade knife out and threatened to use it on me if I didn't give him all my money. I told him that all I had was $.39. He demanded that I give it to him or he would cut me. Which I did. I was so angry and scared I started crying. To think that this 17-year-old, 6ft. tall guy would have the nerve to hold up an innocent paperboy with a knife for $.39. He took off on his bike like a rocket.

I went home and told my mother. She called the police. They came to the house and made out a report. The next week another paperboy was robbed by the guy that fit the description of the guy that robbed me. Only this time he got over $200. The following week he struck again. Except this time, he got a surprise. Teddy Chase was collecting on his route on West 7th St. when he was confronted by the robber. What the robber didn't know was that Teddy Chase's father was hiding in the shadows. Mr. Chase was a big burly guy. He was a lineman for Pennsylvania Electric. Mr. Chase grabbed this guy and beat the daylights out of him. He dragged the guy to his truck and took him to the Police Station on 5th St. The police called my mother asking that we come down to the station and identify the robber. We went there and confirmed that he was the one who robbed me of $.39. He was sent to reform school.

At the time I was delivering papers, there were two newspaper publishing companies in Erie. One was the Erie Times and the other was the Erie Dispatch. I delivered for the Erie Dispatch. My counterpart Jim, (who was about two years older than me), delivered for the Erie Times. We both delivered papers on West 8th Street from Myrtle Street to State Street. We were always competing for new subscribers. It got to the point that Jim was starting to get angry with me because I was picking up some of his customers. One day he started chasing me and threatening to beat me up. He chased me down the hill to Frank Porreco's Deli on the northeast corner of 8th and Myrtle. I ran inside panting and wheezing. At the time Lou Porreco a nephew of Frank's was working in the store part time while going to Gannon University. Lou asked me what was going on? I told him that Jim was going to beat me up for taking some of his customers. Lou said "We'll see about that!". He went out of the store and chased Jim. Lou caught him just up the street. I don't know what Lou told him, but Jim never bothered me again. In fact, over time Jim and I became good friends. Thank you, Lou Porrico!

When I first talked to my mother about getting a paper route she was concerned that if I made too much money they would take the monthly "Mothers Assistance" away. So when she and I met with the Newspapers District Manager she told him about her concern. He assured us that the newspaper (Erie Dispatch) would not say anything to the state if they came around to check. In the summer of 1952 my mother got a letter from "Mothers Assistance" stating that they had been to the newspaper and found that I had been delivering papers for four years, making $6.00 a week. Since she had not reported it, they were disqualifying her for Mothers Assistance and she had to pay back $250.00. That is how closely Welfare was controlled back then. It didn't seem fair. That was one of the big lessons I learned early: Life isn't fair. Especially since I didn't make $6.00 a week and was lucky to make $3.00 to $4.00. But we didn't win that argument. My Mother told the case worker that she could only pay $.50 a month. Every month she would put a $.50 cent piece in an envelope and mail it off to them.

I remember when I was in my second year in the Navy my mother wrote me a letter telling me that the "Mothers Assistance" bill was down to $22.50. At that point I had completely forgotten about it. I felt bad knowing that she had continued to pay that all those years when really, I should have been paying. To clear my conscience, I sent her a check for $25.00 so she could pay it off.

CHAPTER 7

The Neighborhood

The house at 343 West 4th Street between Myrtle Street and Chestnut Street was in the Northwest section of the city of Erie, better known as the Fourth Ward. The city of Erie was laid out very well. The East and West streets are numbered starting at the bay front. The North and South streets have specific names.

State Street is the Main street. West of State Street the streets are named after trees. Peach, Sassafras, Myrtle, Chestnut, etc. The Streets east of State Street are named after Countries. French, Holland, German, etc.

Our neighborhood was quite a mixed bag as far as nationalities were concerned. From West Second Street and Chestnut Street to West Second to Cherry Street was all black families. Many of these families were third and fourth generation families born and raised in Erie. Others had emigrated from Mississippi, Alabama and Georgia in the 1930's and 1940's. Erie was where the work was, and color didn't matter to most folks. From Third Street south to Fifth Street was a mix of Finns, Swedes, Danes, Portuguese, and Polish. West 16th, 17th, 18th, and 19th was Little Italy. The south side of Erie was mostly German. On the Northeast side was the Russians and people from the Balkans. The Southeast Side was mostly Polish. The neighborhoods were clannish and spoke their native tongue. There were music and talk shows on the radio during the week-ends that were geared to various ethnic groups. There was the German Hour, which I would listen to each Saturday morning when I was taking German language course in high school. Our teacher told us that it would help us to speak fluent German. What we were learning was called High Deutsch. If we were in Germany and spoke German the way we were being taught we would be laughed at, since they don't talk like that.

Then there was the Italian Hour, the Russian Hour and the Polish hour. I would listen to the Polish Hour and pick up a few words. But for me it was a difficult language.

Our neighborhood spoke English. The people in my Dad's neighborhood on the far west end of third street were all Finns. When my dad started school, he could barely speak English. (Although he was born in this country). They spoke Finnish at home and the kids in the neighborhood all spoke Finnish for the most part. He eventually became bi-lingual. I always thought he was cool because he would be speaking English to my Mom and turn to his Mother and speak in Finnish.

During World War II My Grandmother (Holmstrom) Komula, Aunt Aina (Holmstrom) Makala, and Aunt Wilma (Holmstrom) Nutter were neighborhood organizers for Finland. They would have meetings at the Finnish Lutheran Church on 2nd Street just east of Plum Street on Wednesday evening once a month. There was an Itinerant Lutheran Minister who would come in from Ashtabula, Ohio. He would have Church service in Finnish. Then the Finnish neighbors and friends would bring clothing, shoes, boots, gloves, coats, hats and prepackaged food items, to be packed and sent to Finland. At the time Finland was fighting the Russians on the eastern front and the Germans on the southwestern front. The Finns were kicking butt on both fronts. Eventually the Russians and Germans gave up on Finland and went to war with each other. And we all know how that turned out.

These women were heroes. There is a book written about them and other outstanding women of Erie County Pennsylvania.

I can remember going to these functions at the Finnish Lutheran Church with my mother and sisters. My dad would already be there. Mom would always get upset because everybody was speaking Finnish. My mother would tell my dad that she was sure that they were talking about her. He would try to convince her that they weren't. Then she would say, "Then why don't they speak English, this is America". Couldn't argue with that.

But the Finn's like other ethnic groups didn't want to lose their national identity. It was a bit comforting for them to speak in Finnish among themselves.

The thing that I remembered most as a small child was the smells. They would be brewing rich black coffee. Along with that the aroma of fresh homemade baked kuchens, cupcakes and cookies. The combination was wonderful.

My Grandma (Holmstrom) Komula tried to teach me to speak Finnish, but it was very difficult. Finnish is not a Germanic language. German, Swedish, Dutch are more Germanic. Finnish language and Hungarian are very similar.

I wasn't very close to that grandma and didn't see her a lot. She was bed ridden for the last 3 or 4 years of her life. It was hard for her to have visitors.

I do recall my grandma and Aunt Wilma ran a Finnish steam bath and massage parlor on the corner of Second and Cascade Streets in Erie. They had a very good business. Many important people went there. The patrons would get all steamy hot in the sauna and then go out in the snow and roll around, (crazy Scandinavians). They also did massages. After my grandma got sick they closed the steam bath. Aunt Wilma continued doing massages in her home at 220 West 22nd Street in Erie.

I recall going to my Grandma (Holmstrom) Komula's during the

Christmas holiday and she would be baking breads, rolls, cookies and cinnamon kuchens (cakes) from old Finnish recipes. That was a wonderful smell that said it's Christmas. These recipes were in my grandmother's head. Nothing written down. My aunts would do the same from memory. But unfortunately, that is all lost. The next generations just didn't seem to be interested.

My grandma's maiden name was Honkula. It was told by my aunts and uncles that her father was a cousin to Sibelius the world-renowned Finnish composer. My grandmother also did crocheting. She would be sitting in her easy chair, crocheting and nodding off. But her hands would keep on going and never drop a stitch.

Now that I've told you about my Grandmother (Holmstrom) Komula, I would like to tell you what I know about my Grandmother Schauble.

Born Bertha May Boch on April 6th, 1893 in Berwick, PA. She was the only child of George and Elvira (Parks) Boch. Elvira died when Bertha was 15 years old. That hit her particularly hard since she was very close to her mother. That left Bertha to take over as head of household. She took care of the house, did the laundry and prepared meals. She grew up very fast.

Gram told a story about when her mother was still alive. They had taken in a little girl with blonde hair. Apparently, the girl had been abandoned by her parents and was just wondering the streets of Berwick, PA. It sounded like the girl was maybe 5 or 6 years old. She was given chores to do around the house to earn her keep. One day there was an orange on the kitchen table that came up missing. No one knew what happened to it. When they confronted the little girl about it, she said that she didn't know what happened to it. George and Elvira concluded that the little girl had eaten the orange and was lying about it. So, they put her back out on the street. Gram would always end the story by saying "I've always wondered what ever happened to that little girl. She was like a little sister to me".

A few years after her mother passed her dad decided to move to Erie, PA where he could find work. Later he moved back to Berwick and would marry a woman by the first name of Amanda. From what Gram told me, she didn't much care for the woman and was very angry with her dad when they married. They didn't talk or see each other for a long time.

Uncle Earl told me that he could remember when he was about 9 years old, he was playing in the back yard adjacent to the alley when this strange man came down the alley and asked if Bertha lived there. Earl had no idea who the man was, but he said yes, and the man walked to the back door and knocked. His mother came to the door, looked at the man and started crying. It was her dad, George. She invited him in and they talked. Since Earl didn't know who the man was it was apparent that she had not seen her father for many years.

George had moved back to Erie and was looking for work. Somehow, he scraped some money together and bought a truck. He would go down to the foot of State Street and buy fish fresh off the boats. Then he would go out into the country side south of Erie and sell the fish to people in the rural areas. He got very busy and hired Ralph to help him.

George and Amanda had several children together. I only knew of Donald Boch. He would stop at Grams house every once in a while. Usually when he had been drinking. His visits would frustrate my grandmother. She didn't much care for him since he was the result of a marriage that my grandmother resented. Donald was a bit retarded and when he visited he would repeat himself time after time. Then once he was in the house it was hard to get him to leave.

Bertha married Louis Schauble in 1911 in Erie. PA. Together they had four children. Ralph in 1912, Ruth in 1916, Earl in1918 and Helen in 1921. Louis Schauble was a plumber by trade and worked hard.

Ralph had a severe asthma problem. The family doctor recommended that they move to an area where the climate was less humid. So, they packed up and moved to Wichita Falls, Texas.

My mother told me a story about their trip to Texas. They had stopped in a small town on the way. Her dad parked the truck on a hill. He told them all to wait in the truck while he went into a drug store for medicine. While he was in there the parking brake let loose and the truck started rolling down the hill. Ralph who was about 14 at the time had enough sense to jump out of the truck. Running far enough ahead of it to pick up a rock and jamming it under the front wheel of the truck bringing it to a stop. In the process he broke his hand. But he saved everybody from serious injury.

Ralph was always a hero to my mother. She often told the story about the time they went to the circus in Erie. During the show a fire broke out in the big tent. The fire and smoke moved fast, and everyone panicked. The crowd was rushing for the exits. There was pushing and shoving. Kids were falling down and getting trampled. Ralph pulled my mother, Earl and Helen together and held them to the tent wall away from the main crowd. Then slowly walking them toward the exit to safety. Fortunately, they did not get hurt. Others were not so fortunate.

Somewhere in the mid-1920's Bertha and Louis broke up. They never divorced, they just separated. Gram raised the kids and got some financial support from Louis.

I was recently talking to my Uncle Earl. He made the comment that one thing he could never understand was why his dad was so mean to his mother. He didn't elaborate, but it was curious to me as to what he meant and what was behind it.

About 1932 Bertha met Lane (Pink) Weindorf. He had just retired from the Pennsylvania Railroad. Eventually they moved in together in a house on Walnut Street between Third and Fourth Street. They never married but I always considered him to be my step-grandfather. Later they moved to 343 West Fourth Street and rented it until 1954. That's when he bought the house. I recall as my step-grandfather (Pink) grew older he seemed more and more to talk about the old days. It was like he could remember more about when he was younger than what was going on in his present life.

He was born in Jennette, PA on September 25th, 1873 and grew up in Erie. To me he was like a walking history book and I was fascinated by his stories about old Erie. He told me that he personally knew Joe Root (the guy who lived in a piano box out on the peninsula and almost owned it. Squatters rights). He told me how Joe would walk across the frozen bay in the wintertime and go to the park at North Park Row in Erie and set on the bench, watch people and talk to the ground at the end of the bench. Apparently, Joe was still communicating with someone who had passed away.

Somehow, Joe was proven to be mentally unbalanced and incapable of ownership. So, the State of Pennsylvania took ownership of the Peninsula.

Pink also knew the Kohler Beer Brothers. Joseph and Jackson. Unfortunately, the Kohler Brewing Company was bought out by Schmidt's Beer in Philadelphia and shut down back in the 1960's.

He also told me that when he was young there were a lot of sturgeon in the bay and in Lake Erie. The west end of the bay was known as the "Stink Hole". It seems that the fishermen would bring their catch of sturgeon to that end of the bay and clean the caviar from the fish and throw the fish carcasses up onto the shore. There were tons of rotting fish. Thus, it became the "Stink Hole". Today the lake sturgeon are extinct to the best of my knowledge.

Pink bought our first TV in 1948. It was a Philco black and white 12" round screen. You could barely see the people because of the poor contrast and the snowy background. The TV had "rabbit ears" for an antenna. Every time you turned it on you had to play with the rabbit ears to get the best reception. And yes, you had to get up and go to the

TV, turn the dial to change channels or adjust the contrast. However, at that time there was one channel, Channel 12 NBC.

My grandmother was the custodian of the TV. It would go on precisely at 8:00PM and we had to be washed up and ready for bed before we could go into the parlor and watch TV at 8:00. We could watch it until 8:30. While you were watching TV you were not permitted to talk. It was mainly because the volume was kept very low and you wouldn't be able to hear. My grandfather believed that if you had the volume too high it would wear out! Later I got to thinking that it was his secret plan to keep it low, so we wouldn't be talking during the program.

Pink was very protective of his TV. He re-drilled the holes in the end of the TV plug to make them big enough, so he could put a small lock through them. Then while Pink and Gram were out we couldn't play the TV. Sister Jan figured that one out real quick. She took a bobby pin and opened the lock. We watched TV a lot.

When they got home, Pink would immediately go to the TV and put his hand on it to see if it was warm. But we suspected he would do that, so we had turned it off in plenty of time for it to cool down. We thought we were so clever.

He lived through two major depressions, the Depression of 1876 and the Depression of 1929. As a result, he never trusted the banks. He would keep a small amount of money in the bank but the bulk of it he kept hidden at home. He always believed in having two of everything. He had two houses and two cars. Just in case he would somehow lose one of them he always had a back-up. He worked for the Pennsylvania Railroad as a car inspector, retiring in 1932 (eight years before I was born).

CHAPTER 8

School Days

I went to Burns Elementary School K thru 6th grade. The School was located on West 5th Street between Chestnut Street and Walnut Street. I always had a tough time in school primarily because I couldn't read very well and had trouble comprehending. As I think about it now, I should have been held back a year. I was not mature enough for first grade. But instead I would just barely make it and get pushed on to the next grade. I had just turned five years old in June and still a bit immature. (not quite ready for school but I got through)

Miss Quintin was the kindergarten teacher. As a five-year-old, she struck me as a skinny wrinkled old lady that looked like the witch in the "Wizard of Oz". She used to pull the old switch and bait on kids with their lunches. She would bring some old cheese sandwich and convince some innocent kid that ham was not good for him and that cheese was better and then trade sandwiches.

My sister Jan gave me an interesting update sometime back in 2006 and told me that there was an obituary in the Erie Times that Miss Quintin passed away at age 97. I thought, "wow" she looked old in 1945. I guess ham sandwiches weren't so bad for you after all.

First grade was fun. I had Mrs. Chambers. She was pretty and always very nice. This is where we started to learn the alphabet, sounds and reading. I had a lot of trouble reading. Mrs. Chambers worked with me and I passed. (But just barely). Truth be known I struggled with reading almost all the way through school. In retrospect I know I should have been held back in those early years.

Arly Dahl was a good friend to my mother. She was especially good company for my mom after my dad died. She would stop once or twice a week just to see how my mom was doing and visit for an hour or so. I was in love with her. She was a beautician and always was made up and looked like a movie star. Beautiful! One time I recall, I must have been 8-years old. It was a Saturday afternoon and my mom told me to take my weekly bath. So like a good little soldier I went and took my bath. While was drying off I bent over to dry my feet and touched the side-arm heater with my left butt-cheek. Yeow! I was in such pain I panicked and took off running nude through the house screaming and looking for my mother. She was in the front living room talking with Arly. (Apparently Arly had come in while I was in the bathroom). I didn't know whether to cry, hide, cover up or run the other way. Talk about mixed emotions. The burn was pretty bad. About 3" in diameter and deep. It sure made it difficult to sit. My mother took me back to the bathroom and patched me up as best as possible. Back then it was believed that butter was the best treatment for a burn if you didn't have Vaseline. The salt in the butter had a healing effect. When I went to school on the following Monday, I especially had difficulty setting on the hard, wooden seats. Mrs. Webb (my second-grade teacher) noticed I was squirming and not sitting up straight. I told her in front of the class that I had a burn. But I didn't specify where I had a burn. Everybody laughed anyway. She asked no more questions. At recess, Mrs. Webb took me to the school nurse (Mrs. Quigley) and had her look at the burn. She cleaned the area and put some ointment on it and added a bandage. I also had to explain to her how it happened. It was embarrassing to say the least. But they were compassionate and very understanding.

My time at Burns School was memorable. I got hassled a lot by the bigger guys. I was small and skinny, but wiry in grade school. I always seemed to be the school punching bag. I remember in fourth grade it got so bad I didn't want to go to school. I would tell my mother that I was sick to my stomach, had a headache or whatever lame excuse I could come up with. I finally told her about the problem. She went to the school and talked to the principle Mr. Scarpetti and complained. He was a good guy and immediately got involved and straightened a few people out. The rest of the year everything quieted down. On the other hand, I made a lot of good friends that lasted for a lifetime. John Heitzman, Rich Gloss, Bart Fratus, Barbara Lee, John (Jack) Keefe, Phillip Williams, Patty Porath, Reggie Stonewall, Bob Mucha, Phyllis Simms, James (Mickey) Atkinson, Alice and Vivian Jones, Esker and James Smith (aka Big man and Little Man), Pete Horton, Mike Simmons and Patty Mountain. Although John and Rich have passed away I still see the rest of the gang at class reunions.

I think it was 1950 when I was in 5th grade there was an epidemic of ring worm on the scalp. It was city wide. The kids that got it had to have their head shaved so it could be treated. There was some kind of ointment that was applied and then they had to wear a white stocking cap. It was very contagious. About a third of the kids in my 5th grade class of 25 were affected, girls and boys alike. I was one of the fortunate ones and never got it. About a month after the outbreak the city health inspectors determined that the kids were getting the ring worm from the seat backs in the movie theaters. The seats were decontaminated throughout the city in hopes of containing the epidemic. The schools put out a word of caution if you go to the movie theater don't rest your head on the back of the seat. Strangest thing is; I still will not do that even today. Another thing that I thought was strange was that some of the kids had curly, wavy hair when it grew back. I was envious!

After elementary school I went to Gridley Jr. High School (7th, 8th, and 9th grades) located on Sixth and Liberty Streets in Northwest Erie from 1952 to 1955. From there I went to Strong Vincent High School (10th, 11th, and 12th grade) located on West 8th Street in West Erie from 1955 to 1958. I graduated with B's and C's. I wasn't an outstanding student, but I did OK. Art, History, German, Science and English were my favorites. Higher math like Algebra, Trig and Calculus were not so good.

The taunting started up again in 6th and 7th grade with the upper classmen. Six or seven guys would grab me and force me head first into the big waste barrel in the boys room. Or they would pick me up, set me on the water fountain and turn it on. Then I'd have to go to class with my pants all wet and be teased and poked fun of, since it looked like I had an accident. I can say one thing, I gave them one terrific fight before they got the best of me.

I guess somethings never change. That kind of juvenile nonsense still goes on today. It apparently makes the big guys feel bigger in their feeble little mind at that age. Fortunately, for me, that stuff stopped after 7th Grade. I guess those people started to grow up at that point.

Gridley Jr. High was a great school. Here is where I started to take a more serious look at education and girls. I made even more friends there. I also learned that there were two West Fourth Streets. One was where my neighborhood was at 4th and Chestnut Streets where most of the people were working class stiffs. The other West Fourth Street was farther west on the other side of Goose Creek around Shawnee and South Shore Drive. Most of the kids from that area were decent and amiable. However, there were some that put on the airs and projected that they were so much better than you. For the most part we pretty much ignored those folks.

Cousin Ralph was 14 and I was13 when we became altar boys at the Episcopal Church on the west side of Liberty Street between 9th and 10th streets. We went to confirmation classes and were confirmed there by Father Orvis. Shortly after that we were asked to be altar boys. It was interesting to learn about the alter and to understand the meaning of the various stages of the service. It was important that you were in the right place at the right time during the service so the it all flowed properly. Then when there was Communion we were responsible for getting the bread and wine to the servers at the alter railing. We also took care of the maintenance of the alter on Saturday morning. We replaced candles, polished the brass work, and dusted and polished the alter. We were Alter Boys for about a year-and-a-half then it was time to move on and let some of the younger kids take a turn.

In seventh, eighth and ninth grade, I had Mr. Edwards for homeroom. He was tough but fair. I knew from watching, that you didn't want to cross him. One of my classmates was Charlie Carter. He was kind of a loose cannon. He'd do anything for a laugh. I don't know exactly what he did that morning, but Mr. Edwards came down the aisle and grabbed Charlie by the back of his neck and picked him up out of his seat and tossed him down the aisle to the front of the room like a rag doll. There he picked him up and pushed him through the door into the hallway. Our classroom was on the fourth floor in the back end of the school. Mr. Edwards pushed Charlie down the stairs to the first landing. By this time everybody in our room was out in the hallway to watch. Mr. Edwards glared at us and told us to get back to our seats. Then he ran down the steps and picked Charlie up and marched him down to the principal's office. We didn't see Charlie for the rest of the day. Mr. Edwards came back to the room, calmly took roll call and sent us on to our next class. It was very quiet in our homeroom for the next couple days. We never did find out what Charlie had done. He wasn't talking and of course Mr. Edwards never said a word. It was a very demonstrative lesson. "Sit down and shut up or you're next."

On the other hand, Mr. Edwards had a calmer side. I had him for fifth period World History. I liked history, especially American History. I got along with him just fine. The only thing that made us guys nervous about him was when he would talk to you one on one he would massage the back of your neck. Creepy. None of us cared for that. But you didn't want to say anything and get him into an uproar. So you would just slowly ease away from him nodding your head in agreement with whatever he was saying.

Seventh grade went well as far as the classes, grades and tests. I had English, Math, Wood Shop, Gym, World History and Civics (Problems of Democracy).

At lunch time we would gobble our lunch down in the cafeteria and head for the gym and play basketball for a half hour. One day, a ninth grader joined in our game. My team and I were doing pretty good against these upper-class men. I took a shot from about 10 feet out. The ball hit the edge of the rim and bounced back and hit the ninth grader in the face knocking his glasses off and breaking the frames in half. He went nuts on me. He kept saying that I did that on purpose and he was going to beat me to a pulp. He said he was going to sue my parents. The teacher monitor broke it up and took us to the principal's office. Mr. Jamison was the principle at the time. He was very quiet and laid back. He took control of the situation and got everybody calmed down. He told the ninth grader to have his parents get the glasses fixed and bring the bill to him. (Fortunately, the lenses were not broken). Mr. Jamison would then work out how my mother would pay the bill. Later that week, the ninth grader brought the bill to Mr. Jamison. It was $15.00. He called me down to the office and asked me to take the bill to my Mother. When I did, my mother got very upset. "We don't have that kind of money!", she cried. "I don't know what I'm going to do."

I went back to school and told Mr. Jamison. He was very understanding. He told me that he would pay the bill, but we would have to pay him back a couple bucks a week. What a relief that was, especially to my mom. Between my mother and myself we managed to get the money back to him in three weeks.

In eighth grade, I took a greater interest in American History. I had American History with Mr. John Gillespie. He was quite a teacher. I could have sat and listened to him all day. He was the kind of teacher that would close the book and tell you all about American History. He said he could do this because he lived through most of it. We figured he must be about 200 years old! Seriously, he was a good teacher. He held my interest, I was fascinated, and I learned a lot.

I remember going to the Erie Public Library on French St. and South Park Row on Saturday morning and spending hours going through Life Magazines from 1922 to 1954. Just basically studying the modern history in pictures. It was fascinating to me.

My cousin Ralph was in ninth grade and belonged to the Jr. Hi Y Club (an in-school club) sponsored by the local YMCA. Mr. Gillespie was the teacher councilor to the club. In order to join, you had to be an eighth or ninth grader. But somehow Ralph convinced the club membership and Mr. Gillespie to let me in the club as a seventh grader. I was voted in and belonged for three years. It was a great club. We had dances, swimming parties, (with girls), camp outs and various civic projects. Projects like Spring clean-up at the Peninsula and other local parks. In ninth grade I was elected President of the Club. It was quite an honor. That was my first experience at leadership. I quickly learned that you can't keep everybody happy and not everybody is going to like you.

Mr. Gillespie gave the club a project in forestry every year. He had some acreage over in Sherman, NY. In the spring he would buy a thousand pine saplings from a company up in Canada. He said that they were a penny a piece. He would rent the stake body truck from the YMCA and get a bunch of us guys in the club to go out to Sherman in the early summer and plant as many rows of trees as we wanted. Then back at school in Wood shop we could make signs and wood burn our name on them and put the signs at the head of the rows that you planted. It was hard work, a good experience, and we learned a lot.

After we finished for the day, Mr. Gillespie would take us into Sherman Pharmacy and Soda Fountain and treat us each to the biggest banana split you ever saw. That was the highlight of the day. That store as a drug store and pharmacy is still there and open. But the soda fountain is no longer there.

He explained that these trees took up to ten years to mature. The he would sell them for Christmas trees. Or he could let them mature even further and sell them to Hammermill Paper Company for pulp.

When I thought back about it in later years, I came to the conclusion that Mr. Gillespie was in fact a shrewd and frugal Scotsman as we had heard from other teachers.

I had General Math in 7th, 8th, and 9th grade. In the first two years of math I had a tough time. I just couldn't seem to get it. We had a math teacher in 8th Grade by the name of Miss Rodgers. She was a wonderful math teacher. She had a great personality, loved her job and loved the kids. She would have after school sessions for those who were having trouble with math. She strongly recommended that I come to the after-school sessions since I really needed the help. Although I had to deliver newspapers I decided that if I wanted to pass I'd better stay after school. It was really worth it. Not only did she help me and the others to have a clearer understanding of math, but we had a lot of fun in the process. I brought my grades up to a B from a C- and D. During the sessions we had a lot of laughs. Miss Rodgers had a great sense of humor and would get us laughing and carrying on. Some kids would stop in to see her during our after-school sessions just to say hello and chat. She had a big following.

Sadly, things changed. One afternoon during a math session, Miss Rodgers and a couple of the boys got to horsing around and giving each other love taps on the shoulder and in back of the head. One boy got carried away and pinched Miss Rodgers behind. That stopped everything. Miss Rodgers got very angry and upset. She dismissed all of us.

The next day it was a different Miss Rodgers. All business, no laughing, joking or carrying on. The boy who pinched her was in another class. She was never the same after that. What a shame.

I decided in tenth grade to take Geometry instead of General Math. Geometry I could envision. I liked it and did well. Of course, a lot of it had to do with the teacher. Mr. Lubjecki was an excellent teacher. He made the subject easily understood.

English was a different story. I had a tough time with English. What made it difficult was the fact that I was still experiencing difficulty with reading comprehension. So it was hard for me to read a book (required reading) and write a report in my own words. I struggled but eventually it started to come around. The secret was: I needed to read, read, read. That was how you got better at reading and reading comprehension.

I had Miss Gross for an English Teacher. She was beautiful (Looked like actress Susan Hayword). She held my attention and I finally started to get a better understanding of the language. I think what helped also was that I took a course in German at the same time. I maintained a C in German and a B in English.

During the late forties and early fifties our country was in the midst of a cold war with Russia. We knew that Russia had an atomic bomb. They were always rattling their sword and telling us how they were going to bury us. The US Government had a comprehensive civil defense program. Just in case the Russians decided to unleash an atomic attack on us. There were designated civil defense shelters all over the city. These shelters were stocked with canned goods, water and medical supplies.

At first when we had a civil defense drill we were to curl up in a ball and hide under our desk away from the windows. We didn't think that would make much difference. From what we knew about the Atomic

Bomb at that time, we all felt that we didn't stand a chance. Later they had us go to the basement of the school during the drill, which made a lot more sense.

I remember the day the Korean War started. June 25th, 1950. It was summer, and I had just turned 10 years old. I was at Arly Dahl's house two doors west of our house watching a cowboy movie on their TV. (Arly's Dad was an electronics technician at General Electric in Erie. He was mainly working on refining television performance. So we were encouraged to come over to their house and watch TV as much as we wanted.) The program we were watching was interrupted and President Truman came on announcing that he was sending American troops to South Korea to help them fight the Communist North Koreans who had invaded the South. My only thought was, if the war lasts until I'm 18, I could be drafted and sent to Korea. Fortunately, or unfortunately the war ended in July of 1953.

As I recall it was September 1950 we experienced a strange and unique event. On a Sunday afternoon around 1:00 it started to get dark. It started with clouds that were a yellowish color. By 3:00 it was totally dark as night. The street lights came on and no one knew what was happening. The police, the TV and radio stations were as clueless as everyone else. Some people thought it was the end of the world. Later it was found that some people had committed suicide because they thought it was the end of the world. It stayed dark for the rest of the day. As kids, we were young and too innocent to worry about it and started playing hide and seek and other night time games. It was perfect. The next morning it got light again, but the sky still had a yellowish cast. A couple days later it was reported in the papers that the cause for the darkness was the smoke from the huge forest fires up in North Western Canada. It sure scared the devil out of everybody at the time.

In Tenth Grade at Strong Vincent High School I decided to take an academic course geared more towards Engineering. I took Algebra,

German, English, Problems of Democracy (P.O.D.), Science and Phys-Ed (Gym and Swimming).

Almost immediately I found that I was not a math whiz when it came to Algebra. I really struggled with it. Just couldn't get the hang of adding, subtracting, multiplying and dividing letters. But I made it through with a "C". I liked German and as I said earlier it helped me to better understand English. P.O.D and Science were interesting to me and I did well in those subjects. Gym and Swimming were a cake walk for me. All you had to do is show up and participate. I loved it.

CHAPTER 9

Times Well Spent?

When I wasn't going to school or delivering newspapers we all lived down on the Bay Front. My cousin, Ralph Schauble, and I were more like brothers. He was a year and a half older than me and I always looked up to him. Still do. He was a lot of help in making me wise to the ways of the world. If he saw I was being taken advantage of he would tell me "Don't be a sap". Then he would tell me what I needed to do. He kept me out of trouble many times. We hung out together when we were in elementary and junior high school. I was two grades behind him. We used to deliver papers together. We'd do his route and then mine. It worked out that it was faster, because we knew both routes. Then when one of us needed a day off we could be back up to each other.

Sometimes I would stay overnight on Saturday at Ralph's house and baby sit Richard while Uncle Ralph and Aunt Marion went out for the evening. We would watch Saturday Night Wrestling. Of course, we would get to horsing around and trying all the different holds. Fortunately, we didn't break anything or injure one another. We would get up at 4:00 in the morning go get our papers and deliver them. We would be done by 5:30-6:00.

Cousin Ralph Schauble gave me my first bike. It was a Roadmaster.

As the story goes he was delivering his paper route on West Eighth Street one afternoon. He was on his bike and tried to cross the street between two parked cars and ran right into the side of a car in the travel lane. He flew over the car and landed on the other side, breaking his big toe. Fortunately, beside some scrapes and scratches that was the only injury. The bike was pretty banged up. The front wheel and the fork were toast and the handle bars were badly bent.

Ralph told me I could have the bike as is. All I would have to do is get it fixed. I took the bike to Joe Hoffman's Bike Shop on West 8th Street. Joe looked it over and said it could be fixed. It would cost $28.00. I told him that I didn't have that much money, but I would give him some money every week towards the repair. He was OK with that. For the next six weeks I gave him three or four dollars towards the bill. One night I came home, and my Aunt Helen was there visiting Grandma and my mother. I bragged and told them that I had the bill for the bike down to $6.00. I could pick it up next week. My Aunt Helen said "No, get it tonight" and gave me six dollars. She was one of my favorite aunts. She had a heart of gold. I flew up to 8th Street, got there just in time before Joe closed. I had a bike of my own!

Ralph and I belonged to the YMCA on 10th and Peach Streets and spent a lot of time there swimming, playing basketball, and ping pong. We would go to the "Y" two or three times a week. We would leave the house around 6:30pm and wind our way through various short cuts through people's yards, over garage roofs and fences. We always got to the "Y" just in time.

In the summers of the late 40's and early 50's we spent much of our time down at Bayview Park on the Bay Front. There was a ball park, tennis courts, a basketball court and a public swimming pool. For the little kids, there were swings, merry-go-rounds, sliding boards and teeter-totters.

The other day I had a bologna sandwich on white bread with mustard and a cold Pepsi. That alone brought back the memory of those hot summer days when Ralph and I would play baseball down at Bayview Park. Then at lunch time we would go up to his house on Third Street and his mom or dad would fix us a bologna sandwich on white bread with mustard and give us each an ice-cold bottle of Pepsi. To me it was a delicacy.

Some nights in the summer we would pitch a tent of some kind and camp out in somebody's yard. (We were never allowed to camp out in our yard. Gram and Pink would never allow it). We never slept on these camp-outs. We would have a camp fire, cook hot dogs and marshmallows, play some Black Jack and Poker. Later in the evening we would raid the neighbors fruit trees. Everybody had cherry, peach, apple and plum trees. It was high adventure sneaking into someone's yard at two in the morning, stealing fruit and getting back to the camp site without getting caught by the owner or the police.

I think it was the fall of 1953 when Ralph and I decided it was the Halloween Season and time for some pranks! For starters we selected Mr. Denning, our next-door neighbor, to receive our vengeance.

We were out back of Mr. Denning's house in the "H" alley. It was 9:00 in the evening and we had just got back from the "Y". We noticed that there were tomatoes rotting in his garden. I knew that he had just finished painting his house white. So being the geniuses that we were, we put those items together and started pelting the back of his house with rotten tomatoes. We saw the lights come on in the kitchen, so we took off running. The next day I looked at the house before I left for school. It was not good. That weekend, Mr. Denning hosed the house down and it cleaned up OK without having to repaint.

Oh, but that wasn't enough. We felt that there was more to be done. We developed a plan to tear out Mr. Denning's front porch step. We went to the house after dark around 8:00 in the evening and together we started yanking on the step. Only to find that it had angle brackets and long wood screws holding it in place. The more we yanked and pulled the louder the creaking and cracking noise. All of sudden the front door opened, and we were caught in the act. We took off running. Ralph headed for his house on Third Street and I ran next door into mine. Two minutes later, Mr. Denning was knocking at our door. He was screaming at my mother. He knew it was me, he saw me, and he wanted it fixed and he wanted it fixed right now! My mother made me go over and fix it. All the time Mr. Denning is screaming at me telling me what a mean nasty trick it was and how ashamed I should be. Someone could have broken a leg. Anyway, I managed to get the step pushed back into place and went back home. Then I heard it from my mom - grounded for a week.

It was in that same year and still in the Halloween Season that Shirley, Janet, Ralph and I decided to make a dummy with an old shirt and trousers and fill it with leaves. Then we were going to hang it by a rope from a tree limb over the street in front of our house. Then, when a car came down the street we would release the rope and drop the dummy right down in front of a car and scare the daylights out of the driver. I believe it was Jan who climbed up in the tree and rigged up the rope and dummy.

As I recall, it worked once. The dummy was dropped, the car came to a screeching halt and the driver got out of the car screaming and started to chase us. We scattered to the winds. What fun!

Some nights during the summer we would sneak down to the Chestnut Street Pool and take a swim. There was a night watchman (Larry the Cop). Most of the time he slept in the life guard shack. If we made too much noise and woke him up, he would yell at us to keep the noise down and go back to sleep. Larry was cool! Every once in a while, the city police would sneak up and run us off. Since we were skinny dipping it was a real challenge to run and try to get your clothes on at the same time. I don't know of anyone ever getting caught. But they sure put the scare in us.

The Chestnut Street Swimming Pool was located at the bottom of the Chestnut Street Hill across from the water pumping station and railroad tracks. The pool was square (about 30'x30'). At one end the pool was 2' deep and at the other end it was 7' deep. At the 4' depth there was a square diving platform about a foot above the water and measured 5'X5'. On the west side of the pool there was a row of lockers for changing into your swim suit or back into your street clothes. At the north end was the life guard station. If you wanted to swim in the 7-foot end of the pool you had to swim across the pool and back as witnessed by the lifeguard. I made it when I was 7 years old. (I really thought I was "Big Time").

Boys days were on Monday, Wednesday, and Friday. Girls days were on Tuesday and Thursday. The pool closed on Saturday. That's when they drained and cleaned the pool.

In the winter we had sledding on the hill at Chestnut Street. Half way down the hill was a manhole access cover. In the winter, it would get covered over with hard packed snow. It stuck out like a bump on a cow's rear quarter. Then when you did a belly smacker on your sled, you would come down the hill, hit the man hole cover (aka. The Cow Bump) you would go flying up in the air, come down with a thud, and continue sailing down the hill. But, the next trick was to slow yourself down, so you wouldn't go crashing through a wire fence at the bottom on the other side of the road. Beyond that was a ten-foot drop to the railroad tracks below. There was one time that I lost it and the sled went flying out from under me, under the fence crashing to the tracks below. I saw it coming but it was too late. My face hitting the fence stopped me. I ended up with red grid marks on my face from the fence. Fortunately, they went away in a couple days.

Ice skating was great fun also. I learned how to skate when I was 12 years old. After a lot of falling and getting up I got fairly good at it. On windy days I would open my coat and let the wind drive me. It seemed like you were going 40 miles an hour. It would take our breath away.

Ice boats (powered by sails) on Presque Isle Bay were very popular. Riding in the front basket of the ice boat was a real thrill. Depending on the wind you could get going up to as much as 45 to 50 miles per hour. Lying in that basket about 6" off the ice and zooming along was exciting and breath taking. You never got bored down at the Bay Front.

They also had duck blinds on the south shore of the Bay Front. These were built and controlled by the State Game Commission. I never went duck hunting but from what I had heard the blinds were rented out on a lottery basis. If you signed up for a blind it was luck if you got a blind for a day. It was quite expensive.

The Erie Museum: The Museum was located the northeast corner of 6th and Chestnut Streets. It was a stone mansion that was owned by a very rich family and later donated to the city of Erie for the purposes of creating Erie's first museum.

The Museum had a multi-purpose function in that there were many displays in the basement, on the first floor and second floor. Some historical, biological and geographical. The Museum was also used as an educational facility. They would have speakers and lecturers on various and timely subjects.

Every Saturday they had arts and craft classes for children. Shirley, Janet, Kenny and I would go there as much as we could. It was a lot of fun and we learned a lot about working with clay, painting with water colors and weaving. All the kids in the neighborhood were there. It was a real asset to the fourth ward and the city.

On the corner of Second and Walnut Street was the Jensen House. The grandfather and son would buy old telephone poles from Penelec Power Company. Working in their garage, they would cut them up into 15" lengths and sculpt them into duck decoy bodies. Then the smaller pieces would be sculpted into the decoy neck and head. Then they would assemble them into a complete decoy and paint them like

Mallards and Mud hens. I was totally fascinated by the whole thing. They'd let me watch them for hours, as long as I stayed out of the way.

At one time the land at the top of the hill from Cherry Street to Liberty Street was the city dump. That was where the city would put all the empty tin cans and trash that they picked up from the residence around the city. There was no raw garbage. Just trash. We would go down there and play for hours.

We would look for discarded aerosol cans. Then build a small fire and place the aerosol cans on the edge of the fire aimed out towards the bay. Once they got hot enough they would shoot out over the bay like a rocket. It wasn't all that safe. Sometimes they would get too hot too fast and explode on the "launch pad", or the can would shoot off in the opposite direction. (Werner Von Braun we weren't).

There was a 100' hill going down to the railroad tracks and the bay shore. (This area at the bottom of the hill is now the Bayfront Connector Highway.) The hillside was covered with trees and brush. It was a perfect place to play army. It looked a lot like the jungles in the South Pacific. One group of us would be the Jap's (as they were known to us at the time) and the other group would be the American Army. We would sneak around, hide in the undergrowth, pretend to get shot and fall down the hill. It was a lot of fun at the time.

CHAPTER 10

Little Brother

In the late summer of 1949 my brother Kenny and I got to go to Camp Kiwanis out in Sterritannia Township. Our Uncle Earl was involved in Kiwanis at the time and managed to get us signed up. Kenny was 6 years old and I was nine. We were both excited to be going. The camp was to last three weeks.

I made arrangements for Shirley and Jan to deliver my papers. They could collect each week and keep the profits.

When we got there, it was fun at first, but after the second day we got home sick. We just wanted to go home. After a week my mother and grandmother came and got Kenny. I had to stay. Boy was I ticked. But surprisingly at the end of the second week, I was having fun. Our counselors were Miss Kay and Miss Alice. I was in love with Miss Kay. She was beautiful. At the time there was a movie star by the name of Kay Star. She looked just like her. Miss Alice was a good looker too. Both were a lot of fun. We had arts and crafts, volleyball, swimming in Sterritannia Creek. By the end of the third week I didn't want to leave. I was having too much fun. On the other hand, I was ready to go home and see my mom and the family. But when I got home, my Mom wasn't there. It was her birthday and she was out with Vince Sadler. I was disappointed, but glad to be home.

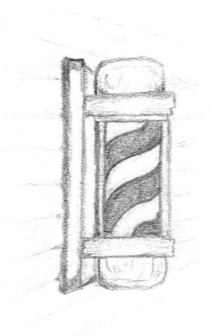

Kenny and I (being boys) needed to get a haircut every once in a while. I can remember my mom taking me to Joe the Barber over on Chestnut street next door to Steinbaugh's Delicatessen. I recall going in there with my mother in the winter. Joe had a small gas burning stove which heated the shop well. But it was a dry heat, so Joe would place a pan of water on the top and arrange orange peel slices on the front grill. Those would put some moisture in the air and give off a crisp citrus smell. Joe was Italian and a proud one. When the mailman (who was Irish) would stop, they would jokingly banter back and forth about their nationalities. It was like they were putting on a show for the customers. They were always laughing, and it was all in fun.

After a while we couldn't afford going to the barber shop. Uncle

Ralph would cut our hair. He was pretty good at it. He did that for several years.

Later Kenny and I would go to Orra-Jean Barber School on 9th Street between Sassafras and Peach Streets. For $.15 they would have a student practice cutting you hair. We got some real dandy haircuts. On rare occasion the student would give you such a bad haircut they would end up giving you a Buzz-Cut just to make you look decent. No charge. But we were young and didn't really care as long as we didn't look like a sheep dog. We weren't trying to impress the girls at that time.

We did a lot of fishing in the bay. Normally we would fish off the boat piers. We'd catch Perch, Sun Fish, Blue Gill. Occasionally we would go after Bullhead (catfish). It was a challenge just trying to get them off the hook without getting stung.

One of the customers on my paper route was a black woman who was a cook for the Green Shingle Truck Stop out on West 12th Street. She lived up on West 3rd Street. We would give our catch of catfish to her. She could take the catfish and skin them, cube the meat, bread the cubes and deep fry them. She insisted that we try some. Delicious. I've had catfish at various southern restaurants over the years, but none were as good as hers. She had a big family and really appreciated the fish. Good people.

There were times that we had to stick around the house to help with the house work or watch Donna. It was fun in the summer evenings around the neighborhood. We'd get a game of Hide and Seek, or play Cowboys and Indians, or just hang out. When we were really bored we would go over to Viega's Mobil Gas Station on the corner of 4th and Chestnut St. and get some empty quart oil cans out of the trash barrel on the side of the building. (At that time the oil cans were made of steel). We would lay the can on its side and stomp on the middle of the oil can. In doing that the can would buckle in the middle and the ends would wrap up around your foot. So we would get two cans, stomp on them and go running and clattering around the neighborhood making a nerve-racking racket. It would drive the neighbors nuts. That fun usually didn't last long.

Sometimes we would play "Pie". There was an area in front of our house that was always in the shade and grass wouldn't grow. It was just dirt. We would take a jack knife and draw a big circle in the dirt. Then depending on how many players there were you would divide the circle into equal portions for each player. Then each player would take a turn with the knife and stick it into the other guys portion of the pie. Then based on where the knife stuck you would draw a line to each edge of that portion of the pie. That then became part of your portion. So whatever portion you had left, you had to keep your foot in your portion. The objective was to win all the other guys portion and end the game.

One summer afternoon Kenny and I were bored and decided to play "Pie". Kenny was doing good in that he had taken a good portion of my part of the Pie. I just barely had enough of my room left to keep my foot on my portion. Kenny threw the knife at my portion and stuck the knife through my sneaker and into my big toe. Now I had seen a lot of movies where the guy would get stabbed and he was dead. I went into panic mode reached down and pulled the knife out (before I died) and took off running into the house screaming. It was quite painful. I pulled my shoe and sock off and found that my toe was just barely bleeding. I wrapped it with gauze, sucked it up and went back outside. I was pleased to know I wasn't going to die.

It was at that point we concluded that to keep your foot in your portion of the pie was not smart. To prevent future mortal foot wounds, we changed the rules and made the game a little more foot friendly.

When Kenny and I were younger we had to go to bed at 8:30. But that seemed so early for us. Shirley and Jan could stay up until 10:00. One night, we were not ready to go to sleep that early. We started horsing around, punching and kicking each other. Kenny put his back against the wall and his feet to my back and pushed me out of bed. That did it. Mom came in and told us to knock it off and go to sleep. Her parting remark was "If I hear one more peep out of you two, I'm going to come back and beat you". She no more than cleared the door and Kenny squeaks out "PEEP". My mother thought it was me and I got paddled. Kenny tells that story today and gets a lot of laughs. It wasn't funny then, but now it strikes me as hilarious.

CHAPTER 11

Ghosts, Police and Sister

T hen there the Ghost House at the southwest corner of the "H" Alley facing West 5th Street. At one time, there was a little old lady living in that big house by herself. She always had the shades drawn and seldom came outside. We saw her a couple of times and thought that she looked like a witch from a bad Halloween movie. Very scary. Apparently, she passed away since the house sat vacant for two or three years. The stories in the neighborhood grew more gruesome about the witch that lived there and the ghosts that were continuing to haunt the place.

As I recall it was the summer of 1949 we were out in the "H" alley playing with Rich Gloss and his brothers John and Ray. One thing led to another and we ended up on the side porch of the Ghost House. One of the windows was broken and had a lot of jagged edges hanging in the opening. We started taking the pieces of broken glass out of the window pane. That's when the dare and double dare started. Eventually we were in the house exploring. There was a back stairway to the up-stairs bedrooms. That was once used as the service stairs. The cook or the maid would use these stairs to serve people in their upstairs bedrooms without having to go through the house to get to the front stairway. We explored the upstairs bedrooms and came to the front hallway that lead to the spiral staircase. Apparently, someone had attempted to restore the house but gave up. They had taken all the shades off the windows and wallpaper off the walls and just threw them down the spiral stairway. Being young and creative we saw it as a super sliding board. What fun! We played in the house all afternoon. Going up the back stairs and sliding down the front. We played hide and seek, tag, cowboys, etc.

At 4:30 Kenny and I went home for dinner. (It was important that we got home by 4:30. If we were one minute late we would be grounded for the night. Mother was very strict about that). We were filthy, so it took a while to get cleaned up for dinner. Mom assumed that we were playing in the alley. She never asked, and we never told. We ate dinner in fifteen minutes and since it wasn't our week to wash and dry dishes we left and went back to the "Ghost House". We played for about an hour and got kind of bored. So we went to the back kitchen window and stepped out. There stood two police officers. Man, they were big. They grabbed Kenny and I and marched us to their police car. They put cuffs on us and started questioning us. "What's your name?", "What were we doing in there?", "Where do we live?", "Who are your parents?", Kenny and I were scared and blubbering all over ourselves. They then put us in their car, turned on the siren and the red lights and took us around the block to our house on 4th street. The officer in the passenger seat got out of the car and went up to the house and talked to the little German lady (Mom). Mom came out to the car and pulled us out. Kenny first and me second. She pulled us out in that order so she could beat my little butt all the way to the front door. Then some more once we got inside. She never touched Kenny. The rational was: I was 9 years old and should have known better than to break into someone's house. Kenny was only 6 and was just following me. I was made to go to bed for the rest of the evening. That punishment was tough to take, especially in the summer. There it was, still light out. All the neighborhood kids were out playing and there I was stuck in bed. Bummer! Kenny had to set on the couch for an hour. Another one of life's lessons. And once again my mom was too embarrassed to go out in the neighborhood because of her juvenile delinquent sons.

One summer afternoon, my mom and grandmother were out shopping for groceries. Jan was babysitting us. Jan was 11 years old so that would have made me 9, Kenny 6, and Donna 1 year old.

I was giving Jan a rough time, being obstinate and just real pain in the neck and lower. I was sitting on the kitchen table (which was not allowed) and looking out the back window. Jan kept telling me to get off the table and sit in the chair. I chose to ignore her. I noticed that there was a small crack in the corner of the window pane. I pushed on it with my finger and a small chip of glass fell out. There was a wet dish cloth laying on the table. I picked it up and tried to push a small corner of the dish cloth into the corner of the window where the small piece of glass fell out. I pushed more and more of the dish cloth into the opening not realizing how much pressure I was putting on the pane. Suddenly, the whole pane popped out of the window frame and smashed to the ground outside. Jan saw it and screamed at me. I took off running with Jan right after me. She picked up the fly swatter that was hand made by my step-grandfather.

The fly swatter handle was made from an old coat hanger and the swatter end was made from an old rubber inner tube. It was a very effective piece of equipment.

Getting back to Jan chasing me: I ran into our bedroom and dove onto my mother's bed and rolled over on my back. At the same time Jan was swinging down at me with the fly swatter and caught me across the bare chest. The sting and shock was so severe it took my breath away and I passed out. It scared the daylights out of Jan. She thought she killed me. About five minutes later I came around. She told me later she had such mixed emotions at the time. She was so ticked at me because I broke the window but on the other hand she knew she really hurt me and felt bad about that. I carry the scar today. In retrospect, I deserved it. I also learned; don't mess with Jan.

CHAPTER 12

The Bowling Alley

In the winter of 1955 while I was in 10th grade my brother Ken and I started working at the Gem Club Bowling Alley setting pins. I would deliver paper till 5:00 stop home for dinner and then go to the Club and set pins. It seemed a bit ironic to be working there since that was what our Father was doing the night he died.

Back then they didn't have automatic pin setters. It was all done by hand. The bowler would bowl his first ball and knock down the pins. As a pin setter it was your job in the pits to pick up the ball and put it on the return rail and give it a push, hard enough to get it down the rail and back to the bowler. Then pick up the pins and put them in the rack above. Then the bowler would bowl the second ball. Again, it was your job to pick up the pins and put them in the rack. Then push the switch and the rack would come down and set the pins up for the next bowler. There was a partition between the alleys that you could jump up on and get your legs and feet out of the way. You had to be fast to get up on the partition and get out of the way or the next bowling ball and pins could hit you and break your leg, ankle, foot or all of the above.

In today's world OSHA would have a real problem with this job!

You got paid $.10 a game per bowler. So, if you had 5 bowlers you would make $.50 per game. $1.50 for 3 games. League nights were

Tuesday, Wednesday and Thursday. Friday, Saturday and Sunday were open bowling nights. On league nights they would have the first league from 6:00pm until 8:00pm The second league was from 8:30pm til 10:30pm. Tuesday and Thursday nights were Men's League and Wednesday was Women's League. Men's League went pretty fast. They usually were done with the first league by 7:30 and the second league would start at 8:00. Then they would be done by 9:30. That meant we pin setters would be out of there by 10:00.

However, on Wednesday Women's League Night it was a totally different story. They had the same hours; 6:00 until 8:00 for the first league and 8:30 until 10:30 for the second. Usually it went well, but on some nights, it went very badly. On several occasions we didn't get out of there until 12:30am. It seems that the first league would start late because one of the players was running late or they would just be gabbing during the game and forget it was their turn to bowl. This would cause the first league games to run over until after 9:00pm. As a result, the second league to start around 9:45pm. Then that set of games would run over because of gabbing and not being aware of the fact that it was their turn to bowl. For the boys in the pits it was frustrating and nerve racking.

I recall one of the men bowlers (we called him Buddy Bomar, a popular Professional Bowler who threw a hard and fast ball at that time) who also threw a ball so hard and fast it was like a projectile from a cannon. When that ball hit the pins, it was like they exploded. You had to move fast and get as far away from the pins as possible. I used to stand on the ball return rail behind the pit when he bowled.

On several occasions I was the only pin setter to show up on League night. I would set pins for four alleys. That was when I was young skinny and agile! One particular night it was Men's League and I was the only pin setter to show. So I agreed to set four alleys. The first league went fast and went well. The second league started early and was going well. Until the guy we called Buddy Bomar got up and bowled.

I was just out of the pit and sitting on the partition and kind of watching the other three alleys, when I heard this loud crack and saw pins flying. One pin flew up and hit me right square in the mouth knocking me off the partition and into the next pit. Just in time for the bowling ball from that alley hit the pins. Fortunately, that bowler only got three pins. I was dazed and disoriented but managed to stagger out of the pits and start down the side to the restroom. That's when I passed out from the pain. The next thing I knew I was setting in a chair up by the bar area with a cold cloth on my face. I thought I lost my front teeth. Apparently, I had my mouth closed when the pin hit me so all it did was crack the enamel and give me a fat split lip. After about a half hour I went back to the pits and finished the night.

On the brighter side of the job was the League Banquets each Spring. The pin setters were invited. It was a great meal and then we would get a bonus from the bowlers. Some years we got as much as $250.00 each. So there were some benefits to it.

One Sunday afternoon I was setting pins for open bowling. This one guy started bowling around 1:00 and bowled all afternoon. One game after another. He was drinking and bowling. In between games he was flirting with his girlfriend sitting at the bar. Around 6:00 he was really ripped. He turned to his girlfriend and said," Hey, want to see my overhand ball." She said, "Sure". So he threw the ball down the alley overhand. I saw it come bouncing down the alley and jumped up and stood on the partition.

The bowling alley manager saw what happened and ran down to the guy, grabbed him by the back of the neck and seat of the pants and dragged him out of the club and up the stairs to the street screaming at him and punching him.

That little trick got the guy banned from the club. It also damaged the alley surface to where they had to have the alley completely re-finished.

CHAPTER 13

Young Man

I n the summer of 1956 my cousin Ralph asked me to go out for Cross Country with him. Mr. Wilkinson, Teacher and a World War Two Army Veteran was the Cross-Country Coach. He was tough but fair. But between working, school and Cross Country it got pretty crazy. The fact that I had taken up smoking (Pall Mall Straights) that year didn't help matters either. So I dropped out of Cross Country.

At sixteen everybody had to get their driver's license to be cool. I figured I'd get my license and then a car. My buddy Mike Simmons convinced his dad to let him take me out and practice diving in his 1948 Studebaker. Then there was Bobby Ziwatski who took me out for a while in his 1946 Chevy coupe with the vacuum shift. The way that worked was unique. Basically, it was a standard shift. But when you went from first gear up to second gear at 25 miles per hour you put the clutch in push the gear shift lever up towards second gear. Once you got past neutral the transmission through some vacuum magic would suck the gear shift up into second gear. Then at about 35 miles per hour you would put the clutch in and tap the gear shift lever the vacuum would suck the lever down into third gear and you were off.

I took my first drivers test in the '46 Chevy and failed miserably. At the end of the driving part of the test there is a hill with a stop sign near the top of the hill. The trick was to come to a complete stop. Foot on the brake with the clutch in and put the car in first gear. Turning signal to the right. Then quickly take your foot off the brake to the gas pedal. Press on the gas pedal and slowly let the clutch peddle out. In doing this you would keep the car from rolling backwards down the hill and move forward without stalling the engine. Well, it was apparent that I needed more practice. All I know is I did what I thought I should, but we were rolling back down the hill backwards. The officer conducting the test is yelling at me to stop the car. Step on the brakes. We swerved off the pavement and came to a stop. The officer was white as a ghost. He made me put the car in neutral gear, pull the emergency brake on, and get out of the car. I walked back to the Administration Building while he drove the car back. He was not happy and stamped "Failed" on my papers. I was very disappointed, but I wasn't going to give up.

I talked to my brother in-law Bob MacGurn (married to my sister Jan). He said he would work with me until I got my license. He showed me a lot and I was thankful. Bob helped me especially with the clutch, brake and gas with a technique that really worked. A week later, I re-took the test and passed with flying colors. So there I was, I had a driver's license and no car and no insurance. But I was cool!

Between school, peddling papers and setting pins at the bowling alley, the days were long, and I sure got tired. But that was the thing you had to do, and you did it. I wasn't the only one. A lot of my friends and relatives were doing the same thing. It was a sign of the times. School and bringing money into the house were more important. It was quite a juggling act. You did whatever it took to turn a buck.

I recall the weirdest thing in 1956. That was when Shirley and Janet moved out and got married, Gram jacked up the rent. I was 16 at the time going to school, setting pins at the bowling alley, delivering newspapers, working part time at G&H Super Market and giving my mother about $50.00 a week. My grandmother knew how much I was giving her so she jacked up the rent. I went to war with my grandmother over that issue. Don't recall if I won that battle or not.

Thanksgiving of 1956 we had a blizzard that dropped 4 feet of heavy wet snow. The storm shut down everything in western Pennsylvania from Erie to down below Pittsburgh. Even the newspaper was closed, so there were no deliveries. My buddy John Heitzman and I went out on Friday morning and started shoveling sidewalks and driveways. We worked all day and into the evening. One guy paid us twenty dollars to dig his car out. He needed to get to work and was desperate. We dug his car out and pushed it on to the street in about a half hour. He was a happy guy. By eight o'clock that evening we had made over three hundred dollars each. That was very good money back then.

On Saturday, we went out again. The newspaper was still closed, so we figured we could still make more money shoveling snow. By then, things were opening up and the snow was starting to melt. We made about a hundred dollars each that day. Still not bad. By Sunday, everything was pretty much back to normal. Then it was back to school, delivering papers and working at the Gem Club Bowling Alley.

In 1956 the Denning Family sold their house to a Mr. and Mrs. Latanzzi. What great people. They had come to the United States from Italy in 1910 and lived in Renova, Pennsylvania. He went to work for the Pennsylvania Railroad as a laborer and had just retired. They moved to Erie to be closer to their daughter, her husband and the grandchildren. They also had a son, Jimmy who was in the Navy.

Jimmy came home in the summer. He was between enlistments and wasn't sure he wanted to re-enlist or become a civilian. By the end of summer, he decided to re-enlist for another six years. He told me a lot about the Navy and how they travel the world. I was very impressed. It helped me make my decision after graduation.

One day Mr. Latanzzi asked me if I would mow his lawn. He said that he just couldn't do anymore. It was too hard on him. He said he wouldn't be able to pay much, but he would give what he could. I told him not to worry. I would be glad to help. Mrs. Latanzzi treated my mom like a daughter. They became good friends.

I started mowing the lawn on a regular basis. The first time I mowed Mrs. Latanzzi made a wonderful dish of homemade spaghetti. There was no meat in it, but it was so tasty you didn't need meat. Then the next time she brought over a homemade pizza, with mushrooms, peppers and onions. Talk about delicious. She should have opened her own restaurant. It got to the point that I would go over and ask to mow their lawn even if it didn't need it.

They always had a vegetable garden out back. Lots of tomatoes, peppers, onions and corn. One day when I was mowing, I spotted a pepper that looked ripe and ready for picking. I asked Mr. Latanzzi if I could have it to eat. He looked at me kind of funny and said sure help yourself. So when I finished mowing I picked the pepper and took a big bite out of it. Wow was that hot. My mouth was burning my eyes were watery and my nose was running. I ran home and got a glass of water. Drinking water only made it worse. My mother gave me bread and crackers. But nothing seemed to help. I had to ride it out. About an hour later I was back to normal. Mr. Latanzzi said that he thought I knew what I was doing. But he couldn't understand why I would want that hot pepper. Lesson learned. I won't do that again.

The next spring Mr. Latanzzi passed away. Mrs. Latanzzi continued to live in the house for a couple of months. But then she decided that the house was too much for her to keep up with and decided to move in with her daughter. She sold the furniture that she wouldn't need. Then she gave my mother an end table, a couple of lamps and a brass rail bed complete with mattress and springs. It was beautiful. The head board and foot board were a bright polished brass in several tones. It was quite antique and in original condition. Mom was so thrilled with the bed.

Not only by the beauty but by the fact that Mrs. Latanzzi thought that much of her to give this beautiful bed.

Whenever I had some spare time in the evenings I would go over to Bud Veiga's Mobile Gas Station on the northwest corner of Fourth and Chestnut and hang out with the boys. Bud's oldest son, Sonny, and middle son, John (Jack), ran the station at night. There would be about 4 or 5 of us just standing around talking about cars, girls, then cars, then girls. We were drinking Coke-Cola and smoking them cigarettes. Big time! Of course, there was a lot of horsing around, like punching each other, teasing and bantering. One night, Sonny and another guy got into it and ended up wrestling. It got a little out of hand and Sonny went through one of the plate glass front window panels. Fortunately, Sonny didn't get cut. But on the other hand, he had a lot of explaining to do. He called his dad and told him what had happened. His dad went up in smoke. Everybody left like rats leaving a sinking ship.

The next night I stopped by the station, but Bud was running it that night. He told me that the fun was over. No more hanging around when Sonny or Jack were on duty. He went on to say that he is running a business, not an amusement park. Fortunately, no one got hurt. He just can't put up with this.

I meekly apologized for being a part of it and left. Things cooled down in the next couple months. Gradually we started hanging out at the gas station again. But we had a much different attitude about the business.

In Spring of 1957 my brother-in-law, Bob MacGurn, suggested that I put my application in for a job at G&H (Gardener and Harf) Super Markets. It was a part-time stock boy position working after school and on Saturdays. I went to their offices and filled out an application. About two weeks later I got an interview with Walter Harf (one of the owners). The interview went well, and I got hired in at the West 12th Street Store. It started out at $1.25/hr. and scheduled for 15 to 20 hours a week. So after taxes you would take home about $15.00 to $20.00 a week. Before I could start I had to get working papers from the State Employment Office. This was required due to Pennsylvania Child Labor Laws. I filled them out, had my mother sign them, turned them in and I was good to go.

I would go in after school on Wednesday, Thursday and Friday work from 4:00pm until 9:00pm. Charlie Leingang and I would walk from Strong Vincent out to the Store on 12th near Pittsburgh Ave.

I really liked the job. It involved checking the shelves, making an order list and then going back to the stock room pulling the stock and taking it out stamping the price on the product and restocking the shelves. Sweeping the isles. Cleaning the windows, packing groceries and taking them out and putting them in the customers car.

The store manager was Larry Sonowski. He seemed uptight and not very sociable. He wasn't there to win a popularity contest. He would tell us what had to be done and we'd go do it. The assistant manager was Ted Palace. He was a younger guy and we got along fine. He was good to work for.

I thought I was doing well. After about six weeks I got called into the Employees Break Room by Larry. He told me that Walter Harf was on the way wanted to talk to me.

About ten minutes later Walter came in, sat down and started to talk to me. He told me that I was not doing the job. That it was reported that I am standing around a lot and not doing anything. He asked me what I had to say for myself?

I told him that I thought I was doing everything I was told. Maybe when I would finish a job I would stand there waiting to be told what to do next. Since I had never worked in a store before I didn't know what else to do unless I was told. He told me that I should just go sweep the floors or take out trash, whatever. But keep busy. I should have known that. Therefore, he was going to fire me. I was shook. I didn't want to lose this job. I really liked it. I just sat there looking at Walter. Then it seemed like out of nowhere there was a figure in a white uniform standing in the doorway. It was Dave Crossman, the head butcher. He was not only the head butcher but he was President of the Union.(The Amalgamated Meat Cutters and Butchers of America). Dave asked what was going on. Walter told him that he had just fired me. Dave said that he can't just fire someone without talking to the Union. Dave sat down and talked to Walter to hear his side and then hear my side. Dave asked me to leave the room for a while and he would talk with Walter.

While I was standing outside the break room, Larry was called into the room. About fifteen minutes later they called me back in. Walter said that he would give me another chance and I was hired back on a trial basis. He said that we would get back together in thirty days and review my performance. Walter, Dave and Larry agreed that if my performance hadn't improved then I would be let go. It sounded reasonable to me. I assured them that I would work hard and do my very best. They also told me that I would be working directly for Ted Palace. So when I was done with a task go to Ted and he will let you know what is next to be done. Then eventually I would gain the experience to the point that I'll know what needs to be done and go ahead and do it. I left the room smiling.

Working for Ted was a pleasure. He was a good instructor. After a while the job became second nature. I knew what had to be done and when it had to be done.

At the end of thirty days I met with Walter, Dave, Larry and Ted. I got good marks from Larry and Ted. They were both very pleased with my improved performance. Walter told me that I had the job and keep up the good work.

If it wasn't for Dave Crossman and the Union getting involved I would have been a goner. That may have otherwise changed my whole outlook on working and life in general.

In the 1950's Pennsylvania still had their "Blue Laws" in effect. The laws prohibited department stores, grocery stores, saloons, restaurants that served alcohol from opening on Sunday. However, the social clubs were permitted to open on Sunday at noon.

I managed to work around those laws. Not violating them but working in line with them. I quit my paper route. It was about time. Eight years was enough.

My schedule at the grocery store after school was Thursday and Friday from 4:00pm until 9:00pm. Saturday from 8:00am until 2:00pm or 12:00pm until closing at 8:00pm. So with that schedule, I could work Sunday, Monday, Tuesday and Wednesday at the bowling alley. I was getting the best of both working worlds and still going to school. Mom said I could quit school when I graduate!

CHAPTER 14

Parting Ways

I recall it was October of 1957 when my Mother told me that she had had it with living at Gram's and putting up with all the things that she had been pulling on her over the years. She said that she was taking Kenny and Donna and moving to her boyfriend Vince Sadler's house on East Grandview Blvd. Since I was about to graduate from Strong Vincent High School in June of 1958, I could move in with Jan and Bob. They had just moved into Georgie Weibler's house across the street on the north side of fourth street. Mom had already discussed it with Jan and Bob. They said that they had a room and it was OK. My mother said that she would give them my portion of the Social Security check each month to cover room and board. And I was to give them $15.00 a week for laundry and food. I was a bit dumbfounded at first, but I finally said it was OK.

I know Kenny and Donna were not crazy about it. They were being pulled out of school, away from their friends and the neighborhood they had grown to know and love.

At the time I could understand how my mother felt. She had been verbally and financially abused by my grandmother all these years and just couldn't take it anymore. So, in a sense it was an act of desperation.

My grandmother was really upset and tried to talk my mother out of it, but to no avail. In turn, my grandmother told my mother that she owed for the gas and electric bill for the rest of the month. My mother refused to pay. Gram said that she would keep my mom's brass rail bed and dresser until such time she paid up.

The move was made. Mom, Kenny, and Donna went to Vince's on East Grandview and I moved in with Jan, Bob and baby Ann.

I continued with school and kept on working at the grocery store and the bowling alley. I thought things were going OK considering the circumstances. But it wasn't working well financially for Jan and Bob. It seems that it was costing them more to keep me than they expected. Mom couldn't give them anymore, so I started giving them $20.00 a week. That helped for a while, but then that still wasn't enough.

My sister Shirley offered to help by taking me until I graduated in June. I moved in mid-December of 1957. Shirley was married to Pat McKinney at the time and had a daughter Karen. They lived in an upstairs apartment on West 10th Street near Cascade Street. It was located near Strong Vincent High School so that worked well. For the most part things went pretty smooth, although I had some ups and downs with Pat.

I continued with school and working at G&H Super Market. By then I had given up my job at the bowling alley. I wanted more time to concentrate on school and give it one last push to get my grades up for that final report card.

CHAPTER 15

Youngest Sister

1958 seemed to be the year of major change. This was the year that I would graduate from high school, join the Navy and start a new life. I had a lot of anxiety and anticipation about the future, as many of us did. Some of my classmates and friends would be going off to college, others into various branches of the military. Yet others would be staying in Erie and try to find work.

School was going well. I was maintaining a C+ and better average. Which for me was good. English and German classes were getting easier. Art was easy for me and I was maintaining an "A".

One afternoon in February I stopped to see sister Jan after school. She was upset and wouldn't say why. She told me to go across the street and see Gram Schauble. So I went to find out what was going on. My grandmother told me that my mother had a baby girl. My mother was 42-years old. How could that be? I was in total shock. Apparently, I was the only one that didn't know or didn't suspect, even back in October of 1957 when all the moves were made. I guess I was too young and too naive to think of my mother like that. I felt that I had been deceived for the last 5 months. I was really upset with everyone. I found out later that even my brother Ken and sister Donna didn't know.

It took me a while to adapt to the idea that I had a half-sister. Eventually

I got over being upset and figured what is done is done. There is no undoing, so move on.

On the other hand, my two older sisters had children that were a year or so older than their new Aunt Nancy. It must have seemed really strange to them at the time.

In a sense I felt sorry for my mom. She had lived through some rough times for most of her life and the last thing she needed was another child to raise at her age. But I guess it was all part of God's plan.

We all loved Nancy and treated her like a sister. So life goes on.

Home life at Shirley's got crazy. Pat was on me all the time about one thing and another. I got the distinct feeling from him that I was not welcomed there. Shirley was fine with me being there so that's what mattered. I just stayed out of Pat's way.

Pat was a used car Salesman working for Kimmel Pontiac on 26th and Greengarden Ave. He did line me up with a car. It was a 1937 Dodge four door sedan. It was in fairly good shape but needed some work on the brakes.

All they wanted was $40.00 for it. So I bought it. I spent nights working on the brakes. Then polishing and cleaning on Sunday's. It was the "Bomb". It had a floor shifter with a six-cylinder engine. It looked like the old guy that owned it before painted the car gray (with a paint brush). I used rubbing compound to smooth it out and make it look halfway decent. It was a lot of elbow work, but the end result was worth it. Finally, I got it ready for inspection and it passed. But then the major problem showed up. I couldn't afford the insurance. All I needed was collision insurance. It was $78.00 for the year. But I didn't have it. I had Pat sell the car. I got $40.00 out of it and a hard lesson in planning and looking ahead.

Work at the grocery store was getting sparse. Because of the recession and lack of work in general, people weren't buying groceries like they had been. In turn, there were some lay-offs at the store. I was lucky I didn't get laid-off. However, they transferred me to the Wesleyville

Store. Since I didn't have a car, I had to take the bus. I would get out of school, walk home and get a bite to eat then go to the bus stop on Tenth and Cranberry Streets. I would then get on the bus and ride to South Park Row into downtown Erie. I would wait ten minutes and get on the Wesleyville Bus, arriving at the store at 4:45PM. I would work from 5:00 until 9:00. Then back on the bus and get home about 9:45. It was tough, but I was still working and doing good in school.

Just before graduation, my art teacher Mr. Grack came to me and said that he could get me a one-year Art Scholarship to Edinboro State Teachers College. From there I would be on my own. But given my abilities I could get more scholarships and grants to finish my four years and become an art teacher.

I was quite honored to think that he would do that for me. I told him that I would think about it and let him know. A couple days later I told him that I appreciated the offer, but I had decided to go in the Navy for four years. I told him that college would be great, but I would have no way to support myself and still go to school. There weren't that many jobs around at the time, since we were in the middle of a deep recession. So the only option that made sense to me at the time was to go into the Navy (before I got drafted into the Army, which was a good possibility). This way, when I got out I would have the veterans benefits and have college paid for by Uncle Sam. I could see he was disappointed, but he said he understood.

I finished the school year with fairly good grades and graduated on June 12th, 1958. There were approximately 235 people in the graduating class. My standing in the graduating class was somewhere in the middle.

I turned 18 on June 3,1958. At the time the Navy had a program where if you joined the day before you turned 18 then you could get out the day before you turned 21. Affectionately known as a "Kiddie Cruise". As you can see by the dates above that didn't work for me. I did four years in the U.S. Navy. It was a positive life changing experience for me. That experience just may be a sequel to this book.

CONCLUSION

Even though I have moved away from the Fourth Ward I am always drawn back to it. That was where I always felt comfortable. People and places that I knew and loved.

Today whenever I'm in Erie I cruise through the old neighborhoods reminiscing about the old days.

I hardly recognize the neighborhoods in the Fourth Ward. I really have to go slowly and look carefully because it has changed so much.

My brother Ken and his son Ken are the only ones I know in that neighborhood.

Ken bought the house at 343 West 4th Street back in 1973. Gram decided that it was too big for her to handle so she sold it to Ken and moved into a mobile home. Ken is a carpenter and has just about rebuilt the house. He's done a great job in remodeling and preserving it.

I always thought it should be an historical site, given its age and history as the Erie Girls Dance Academy. The house is nearly 200 years old!

The houses on both sides of 343 West 4th have been torn down. The lot on the east side where the Denning house stood is now a vacant lot. However, the lot on the west where the Wells Girls lived: their house is gone and replaced by a small condo.

Steinbaugh's Deli and Joe's Barber Shop are gone. Just an empty lot.

Farrell's Grocery Store has managed to survive. Scott Askins (a kid from the neighborhood) owns it and has run it for years.

Veiga's Mobile Gas Station has been torn down. In fact, half of the block from fourth to third streets has been razed and replaced by the Martin Luther King Center. A much-needed asset to the community.

Driving out to the west end of West Third Street and working my way east towards State St. I drive by my Grandma (Holmstrom) Komula's house and Uncle Johns house just up the street from Grandma's house. Then down to Second and Plum Streets where the Old Finnish Lutheran Church still stands. Then to Third and Liberty to the Barber Shop with the apartment in the back. This is where we lived the year I was born. It is still there but looks to be vacant. Then I go over to Second and Cherry Streets and drive by Rich Gloss's house and across the street is Mike Simmon's home.

Looking across Second and Cherry Streets there are now condos that have a great view of the Bay. This is where the city dump used to be. It was a nice change. Turning right onto Second Street going towards Walnut Street I pass Bay View Park on the left. It's still there and greatly improved. The baseball diamond in still there. The tennis courts have been maintained and they have added a couple basketball courts. The swing sets and jungle gyms have all been upgraded to meet the new Child Safety Standards.

I can remember trying to slide down the old shiny metal slides on a hot sunny summer day. If you weren't careful you could leave some skin from the back of your legs frying on the slide. You might only do that once!

Then continuing over Second Street past Walnut there was Pete and Bobby Horton's house on the right and Reggie Stonewall's house on the left. There next to Pete's house was Esker and James Smith's house. At the end of the block was Jimmy Atkinson's house on the right.

Turning right onto Chestnut going south, then turning right onto

Third Street I head toward cousin Ralph's house at 512 West Third. That house is gone but it has been replaced by a newer brick home. Across the street is where Janet Bross lived. Cousin Ralph married her in 1961. Next to Janet's house was Dashes Grocery Store. It's still there but a different name.

Circling around I end up at Chestnut and Front Streets. This is where we did all of our snow sledding. On the Chestnut Street hill with the infamous Cow Bump. Looking down at the bottom of the hill and across the Bay Front Connector Highway I can see where the Chestnut Street Public Swimming Pool used to be. It's all filled in and looks like they are using it as a Parking lot. The old water pump house is still there at the bottom of the hill, but it looks like it is not in operation. I'm sure new more efficient pumping technology has taken its place.

At Second and State Street stands Hamot Hospital. It has almost Tripled in size since I was born there. There is a picture of the original hospital on my birth certificate. At that time, the hospital was a huge stone mansion that was donated to the city of Erie by the Hamot Family for use as a hospital. Today it is one of the major medical centers in the region.

It's been said that you can never go home. Over the years I have found this to be true. The places and people that were there in the Fourth Ward are gone. But I still have my memories.

It was a time when life seemed simpler. We were young, innocent and somewhat blissful. Sure, there were bad times, but we just naturally seem to have a tendency to remember only the good things and the good times.

They say, "It's OK to look back but don't stare too long". I've just looked back over the first eighteen years of my seventy-eight years on this earth and don't regret it a bit. It was a time when there have been so many changes in the world. A time of coming out of the Great

Depression, a World War, the Cold War, the invention of television just to name a few.

I hope you have enjoyed this read as much as I have enjoyed putting it together.

Mother and Father side

Mother: Ruth Leona (Schauble) Holmstrom Age 24 (Age at my birth). Born August 15th,1916, Died August 13th,1964 Age 47. (Cerebral hemorrhage)

Father: Arthur Walter Holmstrom Age 29 (Age at my birth). Born December 26th, 1910. Died December 21st, 1947. Age 36. (Heart Failure)

Children of A. Walter and Ruth L. (Schauble) Holmstrom:

Daughter: Shirley May (Holmstrom) Wagoner. Born April 19th, 1937.

Daughter: Janet Ruth (Holmstrom) Mac Gurn. Born July 31st, 1938. Died August 12th 2016. (Cancer)

Son: David Paul Holmstrom Born June 3rd, 1940

Son: Kenneth James Holmstrom. Born July 12th, 1943.

Daughter: Donna Jane (Holmstrom) Thompson. Born April 19th, 1948.

Half Sister: Nancy Jo (Sadler) Ozimek. Born February 24th,1958.

Grandmother (Mothers side) Bertha May (Boch) Schauble. Born April 6th, 1893 in Berwick, PA. Died October 16, 1983. (old age)

Grandfather: Louis Schauble. Born March13th,1890 in Erie, PA. Died March 3rd, 1963. (pneumonia).

Uncle (Mothers Side): Ralph Elmer Schauble Born July 18th, 1914. Died March 14th, 1994. (Alzimers)

Uncle (Mother's side): Earl Leroy Schauble Born October 24th, 1918. (He passed away in December of 2017 at 99 years old).

Aunt (Mothers Side) Helen Pearl (Schauble) Mitchell. Born March 12th,1921, Died October 29th,1998. (cancer)

Children of Ralph and Marion (King) Schauble:

Cousin: Ralph Lee Schauble. Born January 10th, 1939.

Cousin: Richard Schauble. Born: April 1st, 1947. Died October 2005. (heart failure)

Cousin: Debra (Schauble) Watkins. Born September 26th, 1954.

Children of Earl and Alveena (Pistori) Schauble:

Cousin: Edward Schauble. Born March 29th 1942.

Cousin: Kathleen (Schauble) Pullen. Born February 22nd, 1945.

Cousin: Marilyn Schauble Born November 26th, 1948.

Children of Robert and Helen (Schauble) Mitchell:

Cousin: Robert E. Mitchell. Born September 25th, 1943.

Cousin: Jeanne (Mitchell) Gray. Born May 15th, 1957.

Grandmother (Father's side) Alexandra (Honkola, Holmstrom) Komula. Born February 2nd, 1880 in Finland near Tamperia. Died March 26,1956. (pneumonia)

Came to the United States when she was 16 (1894). Lived in New York City and worked as a child care giver. Came to Erie around 1897. There was a large group of Finnish Immigrants. There she met Arthur Alexander Holmstrom and married around 1898.

Grandfather (Father' side) Arthur Alexander Holmstrom. Born in Finland October 12th, 1872. Died August 13, 1926. The story is that Arthur worked as a carpenter at the Erie Concrete and Steel.

He was hit in the head by a huge log being moved by a crane while doing work at Hammermill Paper Co. It knocked him out. But he woke up and went back to work. That night he died in his sleep.

After my Grandfather Holmstrom died my Grandmother married Renny Komula (another Finn) in 1932. I don't recall him. He died in 1944 .

It was told to me by a second cousin Russell Holmstrom (Ashtabula, OH) that Arthur and his brother Edward came to the United States through Canada. Once they got into the country Edward changed his name to Peterson and went out west. Seems he liked to rob trains. He was caught and hung! Arthur went to Erie, PA where he met Alexandra and married her.

(Side note: I've done some research to find out where in Finland our grandparents came from. I didn't have much luck finding where my Finnish Grandmother lived in Finland. The best I could find was

Tamperia, Finland and that's a bit of a guess. However I found some interesting information about the Holmstrom name in Finland.

It was found that Finland was once a part of Sweden. A lot of Finnish Families changed their Finnish name to a Swedish name because it was considered more classy.

So it could be that my grandfathers ancestors may have done that. Or on the other hand there were a lot of Swedes that moved to Finland and kept their Swedish name. Not sure which is the case. My Grandfather came to the United States around 1896. In my research I found that in 1906 the Finnish Government set up a program called "Finnization". It was a program set up to enhance Finnish sovereignty and the national pride of Finland. As part of this program a family could legally change their Swedish name to a Finnish name. The Research Article shows a list of names that were changed and what they were changed to. The Holmstrom name was on the list. The Holmstrom name was changed to Karikoski. The Karikoski family lives in the city of Juankoski about 300 miles northeast of Helsinki. More research work to be done.)

Aunt: Aina (Holmstrom) Makela. Born: 1899. Died 1965. (Lukemia)

Uncle: John Thomas Holmstrom Born: November 30th,1900. Died July 1984 (prostate cancer).

Aunt: Wilma (Holmstrom) Nutter. Born: 1913. Died 1986 (cervical cancer).

Uncle: Edward Holmstrom. Born: 1917 Died 1966 (cancerous brain tumor).

Children of Aina and John Makela:

Cousin: Pauline (Makela) Lobaugh Born: 1923 Died January 15th 2013. (pneumonia).

Cousin: Sylvia (Makela) Rogers Born 1919. Died 1974

Cousin: Ruth (Makela) Petrone Born 1920. Died 1982.

Cousin: Walter Makela Born 1934. Died December 31st, 2013

Cousin: Joanne (Makela) (married last name unknown).

Child of John and Viola Holmstrom:

Cousin: Ronald Holmstrom. Born 1935. Retired LT. General, Commanding Officer of Fort Sill, OK. Retired and living in Norman, OK

Children of Wilma and John Nutter:

Cousin: Thomas Holmstrom (Son of Wilma Nutter) Born 1932 died 1982.

Cousin: Saundra (Nutter) Lynch. Born 1937. Died 2011.

Cousin: Allan Nutter. Born 1938 Died 1991.

Cousin: Dennis Nutter. Born May 22, 1940. Lives in Erie.

Children of Edward and Julia Holmstrom:

Cousin: Michael Holmstrom. Born 1942. Retired Vice President of AT&T. Lives in California.

Cousin: Gail (Holmstrom) Heinrich. Born 1946. Retired School Teacher. Lives near Pittsburgh, PA

Lightning Source UK Ltd.
Milton Keynes UK
UKHW030621141222
413904UK00008B/972